T0339517

Cambridge Elements ≡

Elements in Language Teaching
edited by
Heath Rose
Linacre College, University of Oxford
Jim McKinley
University College London

INTERCULTURAL AND TRANSCULTURAL AWARENESS IN LANGUAGE TEACHING

Will Baker
University of Southampton

CAMBRIDGE
UNIVERSITY PRESS

CAMBRIDGE
UNIVERSITY PRESS

University Printing House, Cambridge CB2 8BS, United Kingdom

One Liberty Plaza, 20th Floor, New York, NY 10006, USA

477 Williamstown Road, Port Melbourne, VIC 3207, Australia

314–321, 3rd Floor, Plot 3, Splendor Forum, Jasola District Centre,
New Delhi – 110025, India

103 Penang Road, #05–06/07, Visioncrest Commercial, Singapore 238467

Cambridge University Press is part of the University of Cambridge.

It furthers the University's mission by disseminating knowledge in the pursuit of education, learning, and research at the highest international levels of excellence.

www.cambridge.org
Information on this title: www.cambridge.org/9781108812689
DOI: 10.1017/9781108874120

First published 2022

A catalogue record for this publication is available from the British Library.

ISBN 978-1-108-81268-9 Paperback
ISSN 2632-4415 (online)
ISSN 2632-4407 (print)

Intercultural and Transcultural Awareness in Language Teaching

Elements in Language Teaching

DOI: 10.1017/9781108874120
First published online: March 2022

Will Baker
University of Southampton

Author for correspondence: Will Baker, w.baker@soton.ac.uk

Abstract: The central aim of language teaching is typically to prepare learners to communicate through the language learnt. However, much current language teaching theory and practice is based on a simplistic view of communication that fails to match the multilingual and intercultural reality of the majority of second language (L2) use. This Element examines the relationship between language and culture through an L2 in intercultural and transcultural communication. It puts forward the argument that we need to go beyond communicative competence in language teaching and focus instead on intercultural and transcultural awareness. Implications for pedagogic practice are explored including intercultural and transcultural language education.

This Element also has a video abstract: www.cambridge.org/transcultural-awareness

Keywords: Intercultural communication, transcultural communication, intercultural and transcultural awareness, language teaching, applied linguistics

ISBNs: 9781108812689 (PB), 9781108874120 (OC)
ISSNs: 2632-4415 (online), 2632-4407 (print)

Contents

1 The Role of Intercultural and Transcultural Communication in Language Teaching

1.1 Introduction

Intercultural and, as will be proposed in this Element, transcultural communication is not something exotic or unusual but a normal part of everyday interactions for many of us. Contemporary social spaces from urban environments to digital social networking sites are frequently highly multilingual and multicultural. Work places and educational institutions are often globally connected and we work and study with colleagues from around the world. International travel to 'other' cultures for holidays and leisure is an experience frequently enjoyed by billions and a mainstay of many economies. Immigration for economic and social reasons (including war and political instability) has become a common phenomenon. While the Covid-19 pandemic may have curtailed physical movement, it has resulted in an increase in digital communication enabling people to instantaneously interact across physical borders and spaces. Given many governments' reluctance to shut physical borders during the pandemic and their subsequent eagerness to re-open them, it seems unlikely that the physical travel restrictions will remain in place for long. The linguistic and cultural diversity of contemporary social spaces, both physical and virtual, has given rise to a correspondingly dynamic and variable range of communicative practices. The complexity of these communicative practices raises difficult questions about how we understand core concepts in applied linguistics, such as the nature of language, communication, identity, community and culture. This subsequently has implications for how we can best teach language.

To illustrate this fluidity and complexity of communicative practices, an example may help. The following extract is from a study of digital communication on a social networking site (Facebook) among a multilingual and multicultural group of international students at a UK university. It is part of a private message exchange between North (Thai L1) and Ling (Chinese L1), who are discussing the upcoming mid-autumn festival.

North
1. My lovely daughter
2. Thank you for your moon cake
3. It's really delicious
4. I gave P'Sa and P'Yui already
5. and I'll give P'Beau on this Sat

Ling
6. U r welcome, and the mid-autumn festival is this Sunday, enjoy﹋
7. Can u tell P'Sa, she can get her bag back now﹋

(Baker & Sangiamchit, 2019: 481)

While on the surface this interaction appears to be in English, a more careful reading reveals the underlying complexity of the communicative resources used here. Firstly, and most obviously, it is English used as a lingua franca (ELF) since English is neither participant's L1. It is therefore a more variable use of English than that associated with 'standard' English (although in reality that is also highly variable); see, for example, the use of 'gave' and 'give' in lines 4 and 5. Furthermore, English here is part of a multilingual repertoire as seen through the use of 'P' to preface names (lines 4, 5 and 7). In Thai 'P' (พี่) translates as 'older sibling' and is used when speaking to an older person in an informal situation to show respect and intimacy. Additionally, the intonation marker from Thai (') is retained in the English orthography. This is also taken up by Ling in line 7, although Ling is not familiar with Thai. Given the use of this term of address by the two different speakers and the complex orthography, it is not easy, or perhaps appropriate, to attribute this to any particular language. Instead, it may be better to view it as an example of translanguaging that transcends linguistic boundaries. Moreover, and of particular relevance to the discussion here, this can also be viewed as transcultural. We see cultural practices (intimate terms of address) associated with Thai culture taken up by a Chinese interlocutor who is unfamiliar with Thai culture, and communicated through English, highlighting the diverse and fluid links between culture, identity and language. The topic of the interaction is also similarly transcultural, moving across multiple scales simultaneously. While the mid-autumn festival is traditionally associated with Chinese culture, it is also celebrated by many Thais, adding a regional scale, as well as having a global reach as seen in its celebration in the UK in this example. Furthermore, this interaction takes place in the virtual social space of Facebook adding another scale.

This example is presented as typical of the kind of communication that is very familiar to those of us who interact with multilingual and multicultural communities. This will include many learners of additional or second languages (L2) who inevitably find themselves in multilingual and multicultural settings when using their L2. However, the extent to which such communication is featured or even acknowledged in L2 language teaching is questionable. (I will avoid the term 'foreign' language teaching for reasons that will become apparent later in this Element.) Language teaching has frequently ignored or marginalised the cultural and intercultural dimensions of communication, relegating it to a 'fifth skill' (Kramsch, 1993) to be taught only when the supposedly more important other skills have been dealt with. Moreover, when culture is addressed it has traditionally been approached in a simplistic, stereotyped and essentialist manner (Holliday, 2011). The focus has typically been on comparisons between cultures at the national scale and an assumption of the links between a national language, culture and identity. This clearly does not match the multilingual and multicultural contexts and associated transcultural and translingual practices that L2 users are likely to experience in communication. If language teaching were purely an 'academic' subject with no practical ambitions, this would not necessarily be problematic. Yet, there is now general agreement that the aim of language teaching is to enable learners to *communicate* through the language being learnt. If this is the case, then it is crucial that language teaching has a proper understanding of what this communication involves. In this Element it will be argued that this communication is intercultural and transcultural communication and that it is the role of language teaching to prepare learners for this.

1.2 Aims and Outline

The aims of this Element are twofold. Firstly, it will provide an overview of current theoretical and empirical research on culture, language and communication, as well as associated concepts such as identity and community. Secondly, the Element will explore the implications of this research for L2 language teaching, particularly concerning the central concept of communicative competence and the subsequent consequences for classroom practices. However, it is important to stress that this Element does not attempt to provide a single or unified methodology for language teaching. Given the variability of communication and language use, as well as the diversity of language teaching settings, teachers and learners, there will be no single methodology appropriate in all settings. How best to implement, adopt or adapt the pedagogic suggestions in this Element are best decided locally based on the interests and needs of teachers, students and other stakeholders. Instead, this Element is offered as an attempt to promote much needed dialogue between researchers and teachers (Rose, 2019), while acknowledging that the distinction is not always clear, concerning the cultural dimensions to language teaching. It is hoped that this will result in a better understanding of the intercultural and transcultural nature of L2 communication on the part of teachers and, equally important, to greater awareness of the relevance of this to classroom practices on the part of researchers.

The Element is divided into five sections with the first section comprised of this introduction. Section 2 outlines current theories of culture and the relationships between language and culture. Approaches to understanding culture that are relevant to applied linguistics and language teaching are presented. These include culture as product, semiotics, discourse, practice and ideology. The links between language and culture are then considered beginning with linguistic relativity (Whorf, 1939/1956) as the most well-known and influential theory in language teaching. Then more contemporary theories are discussed, such as the language-culture nexus (Risager, 2006), linguistic and cultural flows (Pennycook, 2007), and complexity theory (Larsen-Freeman, 2018). The importance of viewing language as a cultural practice is emphasised throughout, meaning that teaching and learning a language will always be a cultural process. However, languages and cultures are viewed as connected in fluid and dynamic ways rather than fixed national scale correlations. Thus, particular linguistic resources, cultural practices and cultural references come together in varied ways that can only be understood by examining each instance of communication.

Section 3 turns to an examination of theories of intercultural and transcultural communication. It begins from the position that, in L2 learning and teaching, languages will be used in multilingual scenarios to interact with people in 'other' cultural groupings. Thus, when learning and teaching an L2, it is typically for multilingual intercultural and transcultural communication. Traditional cross-cultural perspectives are presented and critiqued for their stereotyped portrayal of cultures and their lack of relevance for actual inter-cultural interactions (Scollon & Scollon, 2001). Critical intercultural commu-nication theories are offered as more appropriate perspectives on the dynamic adaptability of languages and cultures beyond national scales (e.g. Piller, 2011). However, it is argued that intercultural communication research has not gone far enough in conceptualising the fluid links between languages and cultures in the types of complex communicative scenarios described at the beginning of this chapter. Transcultural communication is presented as an approach that builds on critical intercultural communication research but is better able to account for the diversity of linguistic and other communicative resources and their relation-ships to the multitude of cultural practices and scales that may be simultan-eously present in such scenarios. Transcultural communication is characterised as communication *through*, rather than *between*, cultural and linguistic borders, in which the borders themselves are transcended and transformed in the process (Baker & Sangiamchit, 2019). Combined with commensurable theories of translanguaging and transmodality (Li, 2018), transcultural communication provides a holistic picture of communication, encompassing a range of semiotic resources and multiple cultural scales beyond named languages and cultures that L2 users may engage with.

Section 4 draws together the theoretical and empirical research outlined in Sections 2 and 3 to explore the implications for a central aspect of language teaching and learning; communicative competence (Canale & Swain, 1980). Critical intercultural communication and transcultural communication research suggest a more complex view of communication than that usually taken in applied linguistics and language teaching. Alongside a more flexible and multi-lingual approach to language, also key are pragmatics, communication strat-egies, multimodality, linguistic and intercultural awareness. If the aim of language teaching is to enable learners to successfully communicate through the L2 they are learning, then all of these aspects need to be incorporated into pedagogy. Thus, communicative competence as traditionally conceived is crit-ically evaluated and the limitations for intercultural and transcultural commu-nication highlighted. Alternatives, such as intercultural communicative competence (Byram, 1997), performative competence (Canagarajah, 2013), symbolic competence (Kramsch, 2009), and intercultural and transcultural awareness (Baker, 2015a; Baker & Ishikawa, 2021) are proposed as more appropriate conceptualisations of the knowledge, skills and attitudes needed to successfully engage in intercultural and transcultural communication. At the same time, it is also emphasised that there is not one set of competences that would be appropriate in all interactions and that knowledge, skills and attitudes need to be adaptable and flexibly employed.

Section 5 turns to a focussed discussion of intercultural and transcultural teaching practices and the ways in which the research outlined in the previous sections can inform this. The section begins with a brief overview of traditional approaches, acknowledging that culture has a long history as a part of language teaching. However, this has typically involved an uncritical focus on 'foreign' and 'target' cultures with essentialist correlations between language, nation, culture and identity (Risager, 2007). Furthermore, while the intercultural dimensions are now an accepted part of theory, and increasingly language policy, this has not been translated into classroom practices, materials or assessment. Alternative current approaches better suited to intercultural lan-guage education are presented, which include critical perspectives on language and culture, de-centring of the native speaker model, expansion of communica-tive competence and process orientations (Baker, 2015a). This is followed by a detailed discussion of intercultural awareness (ICA) and intercultural citizen-ship education as approaches well-suited to the needs of intercultural and transcultural communication (e.g. Byram et al., 2017; Fang & Baker, 2018). The final section draws together the themes discussed throughout this Element to suggest the core features of a transcultural language education approach. However, just as no one set of competences are applicable to all intercultural and transcultural communication scenarios, so too there is no single method-ology best suited to transcultural language education. Instead, the principles of transcultural language education are offered as a general guide for teachers to develop specific and locally relevant approaches. It is hoped that a transcultural language education approach will inform and contribute to research and teaching that better prepares L2 users for the reality of intercultural and transcultural communication.

2 Culture and Language

2.1 Introduction

In much of this Element we will be discussing the relationships between different aspects of language, culture and communication. It is, therefore, helpful to start by being clear about how these concepts are understood. In this section an overview of theories of culture and of the links between culture and language is presented. We begin with a number of approaches to understanding culture that are relevant to applied linguistics and language teaching including culture as product, semiotics, discourse, practice and ideology. We then turn to the relationship between language and culture and explore linguistic relativity, the language-culture nexus, linguistic and cultural flows, and complexity theory. This section will underscore how language use needs to be viewed as a cultural practice but that the relationship between the two is not straightforward. This will provide a basis for a discussion of communication or, more precisely, intercultural communication and transcultural communication in Section 3. While these first sections will inevitably be quite theoretical, the theories will be linked to teaching, and they form the foundation for later in-depth considerations of appropriate pedagogy for interculturally and transculturally informed language learning.

2.2 Understanding Culture

Culture is a concept that features in many different aspects of both everyday life and academic study. It is part of political and media discussions, a core feature of the arts, and marketed and 'sold' in the tourism industry. It is also studied in anthropology, sociology, cultural studies, business studies, linguistics, health care and education, to name a few disciplines. This wide range of uses to which the concept of culture is put means that a single definition or characterisation is hard to come by. As the cultural theorist Raymond Williams has famously written, 'culture is one of the two or three most complicated words in the English language' (2014: 86). This means that 'there has been more or less a consensus that it is not possible to lay down an "authorised" definition of culture' (Risager, 2006: 42) that would be applicable or appropriate in all contexts. Nonetheless, there are various characterisations of culture that are more, or less, relevant to applied linguistics and language teaching which we will consider here. Firstly, it should be stated that culture is not approached from the perspective of the 'development' of culture and civilisation. So we will not be considering some culture as 'high' culture, for instance the fine arts, such as painting, particular forms of music and literature. Neither will we portray other aspects as 'low' culture, for example 'pop' music, food and applied arts. Neither will we distinguish between particular societies as more or less culturally 'developed' or civilised. Instead, culture is understood from an anthropological perspective in which it describes the way of life of a group of people. Following this anthropological tradition, epitomised by the American Anthropologist Franz Boas (1911/1986), a cultural relativist position is adopted in which cultures are explored on their own terms with no connotation of superior or inferior cultures.

2.2.1 The Product Approach to Culture

The product approach to culture is probably the most common understanding outside of academia and typically found in dictionary definitions such as, 'the way of life, especially the general customs and beliefs, of a particular group of people at a particular time' (https://dictionary.cambridge.org/). From this perspective culture is described as a thing that can be defined and delineated. These 'things' can be physical items like food, art and clothing but also less tangible aspects of culture, such as beliefs and behaviour. Importantly, though, they are treated as being describable and distinct to each separate and unique culture. This approach was prevalent in early cross-cultural and intercultural communication research. For instance, the 'father' of intercultural communication research, Edward T. Hall (1966), described culture through the metaphor of an iceberg that contains all the aspects of a given culture. The metaphor highlighted that much of our culture is out of our awareness or unconscious, just as the majority of the iceberg is under the water and invisible from the surface. This product perspective is very common in language teaching, from the policy level, to materials and teacher and student perceptions (see Section 5). However, this notion can be criticised as misrepresenting culture which is not a static 'thing' at all but rather a fluid and dynamic process. Furthermore, a product approach to culture can result in stereotyped and essentialist depictions of culture in which each cultural group is clearly delineated from another by virtue of their supposedly unique combination of behaviours, beliefs, values and worldviews. Additionally, these distinctions are frequently made at the national scale with culture and nation treated as synonymous. This leads to claims of nation-based cultural differences based on large-scale overgeneralisations. Examples of this include the influential cross-cultural psychologist Geert Hofstede's (1991) well-known assertion that certain countries, such as China, have collectivist cultures, whereas others have individualist cultures, such as Germany. Again, this can be criticised for misrepresenting and simplifying the complexity of cultures in which there will be a large amount of variation both within and across cultural boundaries, especially national scale ones. Indeed, such cultural overgeneralisations may result in the creation of stereotypes that actually hinder rather than help intercultural interactions.

2.2.2 A Semiotic Approach to Culture

A semiotic approach to culture views culture as a system of symbols (semiotics). The anthropologist Clifford Geertz is perhaps most closely associated with this perspective and writes that culture 'denotes an historically transmitted pattern of meanings embodied in symbols, a system of inherited conceptions expressed in symbolic forms by means of which men [sic] communicate, perpetuate, and develop their knowledge about and attitudes toward life' (1973/2000: 89). Unlike a product approach, it focusses on culture as created in interaction as people make use of their shared semiotic resources. As Geertz explains, 'human thought is basically both social and public – that its natural habitat is the house yard, the market place, and the town square' (1973/2000: 45). Additionally, a semiotic approach attempts to understand and interpret meaning as it is created in individual events within their cultural setting. Thus, the researcher aims to create a 'thick description' (Geertz, 1973/2000) of individual events, then connect them to the many layers of culture that give the event meaning. As such, this in-depth, individualised description is the opposite of the large-scale generalisations proposed under a product approach. Given the central place of semiotics in linguistics, it has been very influential in understanding culture in this field. In particular, Halliday (1979) has proposed an account of language as a semiotic system closely intertwined with culture. As Halliday writes, language as a social semiotic means 'interpreting language within a sociocultural context, in which culture itself is interpreted in semiotic terms' (Halliday, 1979: 2). Thus, from this perspective, language is the main semiotic system for constructing and representing culture and, at the same time, language is as it is because of the culture it represents and constructs. We return to similar ideas (Section 2.3.1) when we examine linguistic relativity and the relationship between language and culture. However, despite the more interactive understanding of culture presented in semiotic accounts, there are still limitations in how well it can account for the multiple references and meanings indexed by semiotic resources in multilingual and multicultural intercultural communication (e.g. Pennycook, 2007; Blommaert, 2010; Baker, 2015a). As such, semiotic accounts of culture can still be viewed as overly static and fixed. Nonetheless, this perspective, in which culture and language are seen as interacting semiotic systems, continues to be central in applied linguistics and will be adopted throughout this Element, albeit with a more complex and fluid account of the relationships between them.

2.2.3 Culture as Discourse

Closely related to semiotic approaches to culture and language is the notion of culture as discourse. Discourse is characterised as ways of thinking, talking and writing about particular aspects of the world (Gee, 2008). Taking this perspective, Kramsch defines culture as: '1 Membership in a discourse community that shares a common social space and history, and a common system of standards for perceiving, believing, evaluating, and acting. 2 The discourse community itself. 3 The system of standards itself' (Kramsch, 1998: 127). Kramsch (1998) goes on to explain three dimensions of cultural discourse communities. Firstly, there is the social dimension whereby members of the community interact with each other. Secondly, there is the diachronic or historical dimension through which members draw on shared history and traditions. Thirdly, there are common imaginings by which members share imaginations of what their cultural community is including its sociohistorical dimensions. Kramsch (1998) also emphasises the critical dimension to cultural communities by which members debate, struggle and come into conflict over how the dimensions of culture are imagined and recognised, giving culture a fluid and heterogeneous nature. Scollon et al. (2012) have also put forward an influential discourse approach to understanding culture, which they describe as a discourse system. This discourse system is 'a "cultural toolkit" consisting of four main kinds of things: ideas and beliefs about the world, conventional ways of treating other people, ways of communicating using various kinds of texts, media, and "languages", and methods of learning how to use these other tools' (2012: 8). Scollon et al. (2012) caution that approaching discourse at the level of culture runs the risk of creating stereotypes through reducing people to their nationality or ethnicity. Instead, they propose that researchers explore the many different discourse systems that people simultaneously participate in, such as gender, generation, sexuality, profession and nation. Although we will continue to refer to culture rather than 'discourse systems' (discourse is no less complex or problematic a term than culture, see Baker, 2015a), it is important to recognise that people are members of many different discourse communities simultaneously. This entails acknowledging the complexity of people's identity in which culture is just one of many communities or discourse systems people identify with.

2.2.4 Culture as Practice

As highlighted in the discourse approach, culture needs to be seen as a dynamic and changing process. This is captured in a culture as practice perspective in which culture is viewed as something we 'do', rather than something we 'have'. Thus, from this perspective Street (1993) has described 'culture as a verb' to shift the focus from the static view of culture associated with a noun to the more active and process-orientated view associated with a verb. Like semiotic accounts, culture is viewed as constructed in interactions between people and, thus, culture is intersubjective and interactive. Practice approaches focus not on the systematic nature of culture but on how 'the symbols are created and recreated in "the negotiation" between people in interaction' (Risager, 2006: 49). This also entails that culture cannot be reducible to individuals (as in product approaches that view culture as being in the mind), since it is inherently intersubjective and can only be constructed through interaction. Such a situated and process-orientated view of culture leads to characterisations that are complex, multiple, partial, contradictory and dynamic. Moreover, cultures can also be approached at many different levels or scales as we are able to observe the construction of national cultures, regional cultures, ethnic cultures, work cultures, family cultures and so forth simultaneously and without contradiction. Finally, like discourse approaches, from a practice perspective, culture involves conflicts and power struggles as individuals and groups negotiate existing social practices and norms and possible alternatives. People may choose to identify with particular cultural groups or be unwillingly ascribed to cultural groups, again adding elements of negotiation and struggle.

2.2.5 Culture as Ideology

Power, negotiation and conflict are aspects of culture that are emphasised from a culture as ideology perspective. An ideological perspective highlights that the shared systems of beliefs and ideas that make up a culture also have a moral or political dimension associated with notions of 'right', 'wrong', 'proper' and 'standard'. All groups have ideologies, so there is no neutral perspective, as Gee explains, 'Cultural models are not all wrong or all right. In fact, like all models, they are simplifications of reality. They are the ideology through which we all see our worlds. In that sense, we are all both "beneficiaries" and "victims" of ideology, thanks to the fact that we speak a language and live in culture' (2008: 29). However, the ideologies of groups in power are usually more influential, and other ideologies are marginalised resulting in power differentials in societies. Therefore, researchers who adopt an ideological approach explore how social structures are created through cultures and the associated power relationships they give rise to. This perspective is summarised by Piller who explains that 'Culture is an ideological construct called into play by social actors to produce and reproduce social categories and boundaries, and it must be the central research aim of a critical approach to intercultural communication to understand the reasons, forms and consequences of calling cultural difference into play' (2011: 16). Piller, Gee and others (e.g. Holliday, 2011) all emphasise the importance of critically exploring how culture is constructed, how and who is making use of it. A position best captured in the following questions:

> set aside any a priori notions of group membership and identity and … ask instead how and under what circumstances concepts such as culture are produced by participants as relevant categories … [w]ho has introduced culture as a relevant category, **for what purposes**, and **with what consequences**? (Scollon & Scollon, 2001: 544–5, emphasis mine).

2.2.6 Summary

These five approaches to culture (product, semiotic, discourse, practice, ideological) all highlight different aspects of culture. While the product approach is the most limited in its essentialist and static understanding of culture, it nonetheless, underscores the many dimensions or layers of culture and is the most widely used concept in language teaching. The semiotic approach introduces the idea of culture as a symbolic system and language as central to that system. It also emphasises the interactive nature of culture. A discourse approach underscores the multiple different communities we are simultaneously part of and the role of imagination and shared history in constructing cultures. Discourse approaches also introduce a critical dimension in which power and conflict are part of cultural characterisations. Practices approaches highlight culture as a process and something we do rather than have. Finally, an ideological approach again stresses the constructed and contested nature of culture, with different characterisations of culture in constant competition. From these different perspectives on culture, we can identify a number of core features.

- Culture can be characterised as shared dynamic 'systems' of discourses, practices and ideologies among groups of people

- Cultural groupings and the associated systems of discourses, practices and ideologies are shared in the sense of either self-ascription or other-ascription and so are contestable
- Cultural groupings and systems are constantly in process with no fixed boundaries.

However, it is important to repeat the point made at the beginning of this section that single 'definitions' of culture are not possible or desirable and that any characterisation of culture will be complex, fluid and resistant to simplification. Yet, currently in language teaching, culture is typically characterised by following a simplistic product approach, and the more dynamic and complex perspectives are ignored.

2.3 Culture and Language

A theme running throughout the previous characterisations of culture is the central place of language in understanding culture. However, while the two are closely intertwined, they are not synonymous. We will explore a number of theories of culture and language that help us understand their close relationship and their relevance to applied linguistics and language teaching. These are linguistic relativity, the language-culture nexus, linguistic and cultural flows, and complexity theory perspectives.

2.3.1 Linguistic Relativity

Linguistic relativity, or the Sapir-Whorf hypothesis, is one of the most well-known and influential approaches to understanding the relationship between culture and language. The Sapir-Whorf hypothesis states that 'the "real world" is to a large extent unconsciously built up on the language habits of the group. No two languages are ever sufficiently similar to be considered as representing the same social reality' (Sapir, cited in Whorf, 1939/1956). In other words, we use language to construct and make sense of our world and, hence, how we think and behave (our culture) is 'built up' through our language. Furthermore, according to this theory, each language represents a different worldview. This has led to two interpretations of the theory. The strong form of linguistic relativity, or linguistic determinism, proposes that our language controls how we see the world. According to this interpretation, we are limited to the worldview and culture we learn through our first language. However, neither empirical nor theoretical research support such a deterministic relationship between language and culture. If the strong form of linguistic relativity were true, we would not be able to understand people who spoke a different first language, and things we now take for granted, such as intercultural communication, interpretation and translation would be impossible. Moreover, linguistic determinism does not fit the multilingual and multicultural societies that many people grow up in where they learn to speak multiple languages and are familiar with numerous different cultures. Indeed, it is not clear that such a strong interpretation of linguistic relativity is what Sapir and Whorf intended, and many scholars argue that this is a misrepresentation of their theory (e.g. Leavitt, 2015).

In contrast, the second interpretation, the weak form of linguistic relativity, by which our language influences our thoughts and understanding of the world but does not control or limit it, has received extensive support from empirical evidence (e.g. Deutscher, 2010). Under this perspective, language and culture are still closely connected, but their relationship is not completely fixed or unchanging. As Leavitt (2015) explains, while there may be particular things that a language *must* convey, this does not put a limit on what a language *can* convey. So, for instance, in the English language these take the form of grammatical categories of tense and number. In the Thai language, they take the form of grammatical categories of physical shape. In what Slobin (1996) terms the 'anticipatory effects of language', speakers of these languages need to pay attention to particular aspects of the physical world (time, number, shape) to be able to express their thoughts through language. However, this does not entail that people are 'fixed' into these ways of viewing and describing the world, and people can learn new languages and ways of organising and expressing their thoughts through language.

An important consequence of linguistic relativity is to underscore not just the close relationship of language and culture but that they need to be viewed as similar types of practices. Support for this position has come from cognitive anthropology with researchers, such as Michael Tomasello (2008) and Daniel Everett (2012), proposing that language is a cultural practice that is learnt in the same way as any other cultural practices through habitual group behaviour. Thus, Tomasello writes that 'Language, or better linguistic communication, is thus not any kind of object, formal or otherwise; rather it is a form of social action constituted by social conventions for achieving social ends, premised on at least some shared understandings and shared purposes among users' (2008: 343). Similarly, Everett claims that 'Language is in the first instance a tool for thinking and communicating and, though it is based in human psychology, it is crucially shaped from human cultures. It is a cultural tool as well as a cognitive tool' (2012: 19–20). For Tomasello and Everett, while cognition influences what is possible through language, or rather communication, language is primarily a sociocultural practice. As Everett sums it up, 'Cognition + Culture +

Communication = Language' (2012: 35). This culturally based view of language, supported by theories and evidence from anthropology and linguistics, is the perspective adopted in this Element.

Nonetheless, there are limitations to even the weak interpretation of linguistic relativity. The extent to which a language 'must' contain any particular structure and way of categorising the world is questionable. For example, building on linguistic relativity, Wierzbicka (1997; 2006) proposes that different languages contain 'cultural scripts' which are intrinsic to those languages. Thus, in relation to English and its use as the official language of the Association of Southeast Asian Nations (ASEAN), Wierzbicka claims that there is 'an internal cultural baggage' (2006: 312) so that '[t]he English that ASEAN has used from the outset as its only language ... is, essentially, Anglo English, and it bears the imprint of the cultural history of the English language' (2006: 312). However, such a claim is not supported by the now extensive research on English use in ASEAN. In contrast to Wierzbicka's claims, empirical evidence demonstrates extensive adaptation of English at all levels from grammar (including tense and number), vocabulary, pronunciation and pragmatics in order to better represent and construct local linguistic and cultural practices (e.g. Kirkpatrick, 2010). Furthermore, much of the discussion of linguistic relativity is based on links between national scale cultures and languages, which is just one scale of many. To focus solely on this scale is to take a simplified and essential approach to culture and language that ignores the many different scales and groupings to which we belong and communicate across. Therefore, while linguistic relativity has been central in underscoring the connections between languages and cultures in which they are seen as closely related phenomena, we need to be cautious about the extent to which we apply this link between language and culture to particular 'named' languages and cultures.

2.3.2 The Language-Culture Nexus

A perspective that explains both the links between cultures and languages but also how they can be separated is the language-culture nexus. While this term originally comes from Risager (2006; 2012), what follows is my own interpretation, which is somewhat different from Risager's original. To understand how language and culture both come together and can be separate, it is necessary to distinguish between different dimensions of language and communication. This can be done at three levels: the cognitive level, the sociological level and the ideological level (see Harris, 1998; Mauranen, 2012; Risager, 2006). The cognitive level refers to individual linguistic resources, and here culture and language are linked. Individuals learn to use linguistic resources in particular sociocultural contexts. Thus, linguistic resources build up meanings for individuals based on this, therefore linking language and culture for the individual (what is sometimes referred to as linguaculture (Risager, 2012)). The sociological (Risager, 2006) or microsocial (Mauranen, 2012) level focusses on linguistic practices; that is, how individuals use linguistic resources in communication. In communicative practices, the meaning of linguistic resources is constructed in the interaction and is also negotiable due to the participants' different possible interpretations. As meaning is based on an individual's experiences, the likelihood of similarities or differences in interpretation will depend on the extent that interactants share a sociocultural history. Those that share a similar cultural and linguistic history, for example growing up in the same country, community and generation, are likely to converge in interpretation. Those with very different experiences of using the same linguistic resources are likely to experience more divergence in interpretation. Hence, at the sociological or practice level, how cultures and languages come together is an open question. Finally, at the ideological level, language and cultures are linked through the notion of 'named' systems of languages and cultures, such as the link between the English language and British culture, or Chinese culture and the Chinese language. The pervasiveness of this ideology connecting national cultures and languages is such that it is frequently taken for granted and is a core part of the banal nationalism by which national cultures are reinforced (Billing, 1995). Furthermore, the power of this ideology also means that it influences how people approach and interpret communication at the sociological and cognitive levels and, hence, the misrecognition of national cultures and languages as 'always' linked. However, there is nothing 'inexorable' about this national scale connection between language and culture. As emphasised throughout this Element, and supported by intercultural communication and multilingualism research, linguistic resources can be used in a multitude of ways at many different scales other than the national.

Another useful distinction from Risager (2006; 2007) in understanding how culture and language are both linked and separable is between the generic and differential sense. The generic sense refers to the general notion of language and culture. In this sense, language and culture are always linked since, as made clear in the earlier discussion of culture, language is a central cultural practice and is interpreted from a cultural perspective. However, in the differential sense, which refers to 'named' languages and cultures, such as the English language and British culture, they are not necessarily connected, as explained previously. To continue with the example of English, the extensive research on English as a lingua franca has demonstrated the highly variable ways in which 'English' is used along with a myriad of interpretations and meanings across a wide range of cultural settings (e.g. Jenkins, Baker & Dewey, 2018). Similar conclusions are drawn by translanguaging researchers who view linguistic resources as able to transcend fixed boundaries between named languages and cultures (e.g. Li, 2018). Moreover, to assume a fixed link between linguistic resources and national cultures would be to adopt linguistic determinism, which has already been critiqued as simplified, and essentialist. In sum, how particular languages (or better still, linguistic resources) and cultural practices come together is an empirical question that can only be answered by investigating individual examples of communication. It is this coming together of linguistic and cultural resources in variable ways in each instance of communication that is referred to by the language-culture nexus.

2.3.3 Linguistic and Cultural Flows

The notion of linguistic and cultural flows provides a metaphor for conceptualising how languages and cultures are linked in particular instances of communication. These ideas come from transnational and transcultural flows in sociology and anthropology (Appadurai, 1996; Hannerz, 1996) and explore how cultural and linguistic practices flow through globally connected social networks. Under this perspective, the global scale exists as one of many scales alongside the nation, the 'local' and the numerous other groupings to which we belong. In applied linguistics, Pennycook (2007) discusses transcultural global flows of linguistic and cultural forms and practices across and through interconnected localities. As Pennycook (2007) argues, this does not lead to homogenisation of cultures and languages but rather to re-embedding, adaptation and changes. Thus, a global language such as English can be seen as moving through globally connected networks in which it is constantly adapted in each setting, which in turn influences how it is used in the next setting, resulting in a continuous flow of change. As Pennycook writes in relation to English, '[it] is a translocal language, a language of fluidity and fixity that moves across, while becoming embedded in, the materiality of localities and social relations. English is bound up with transcultural flows, a language of imagined communities and refashioning identities' (2007: 4–5). The ideas of 'fluidity' and 'fixity' are also crucial, since the adaptation and changes these flows give rise to are not limitless. Counter to the fluidity of languages and cultures, there needs to be enough fixity to language for it to serve as a shared linguistic resource between different groups. In other words, for a language to be understood by all who use it, there must be a degree of similarity or shared understanding. Furthermore, as discussed in relation to power and ideology, people are not free to identify with any cultural group they wish. As Pennycook sums it up, '[c]aught between fluidity and fixity, then, cultural and linguistic forms are always in a state of flux, always changing' (2007: 8).

2.3.4 Language and Culture as Complex Adaptive Systems

The final approach in understanding the connections between language and culture that is commensurable with the previously outlined perspectives are complexity theory and complex adaptive systems (CAS). Complexity theory provides a useful metaphor, heuristic or metatheory for conceptualising how linguistic and cultural 'systems' can be both coherent and constantly changing, as well as how such systems interact and influence each other. As emergent and dynamic systems, CAS are continuously reacting to and in turn influencing the environment that they are part of and, thus, constantly in a state of change with no fixed end point (Miller & Page, 2007; Larsen-Freeman & Cameron, 2008). Emergentism is a central feature of CAS by which the interaction of components, or behaviour of individuals in social systems, result in the emergence of collective patterns that form complex systems. However, crucially, these emergent systems cannot be reduced or read back into the individual components, since no one component contains all the features or behaviours of the more complex system. As Miller and Page explain,

> At the most basic level, the field of complex systems challenges the notion that by perfectly understanding the behavior of each component part of a system we will then understand the system as a whole. One and one may well make two, but to really understand two we must know both about the nature of 'one' and the meaning of 'and'. (2007: 3)

Therefore, relationships (the 'and') between the different parts of the system are as important as the parts (the 'one'). Furthermore, CAS are embedded in and contingent on context and so constantly influenced by and influencing other CAS, again underscoring the relational aspect of such systems.

From a complexity theory perspective, cultures are viewed as CAS that emerge from the interactions of the individual members of the cultural group but are not reducible to any one individual. Furthermore, cultures as CAS will be constantly in process with blurred boundaries and no fixed form. Consequently, we avoid static descriptions of culture and simplistic and essentialist characterisations that equate individual behaviours and beliefs with cultures (Baker, 2015a). Similarly, language can be seen as a CAS that emerges from the individual use of language in communication but is not synonymous with any individual's linguistic repertoire (Larsen-Freeman & Cameron, 2008). Accordingly, a description of 'English' as a CAS will be based on the aggregate language use of 'English' speakers but will differ from an individual's language use (Larsen-Freeman, 2018). This is because each user of English will make use of the linguistic resources associated with English in a different way based on their unique combination of histories, settings and purposes. Moreover, following a complexity theory approach, both linguistic and cultural systems, such as 'English' and 'British' culture, are viewed as interacting with other linguistic and cultural systems and so the boundaries between systems are blurred and constantly changing. This can include national scale cultural and linguistic systems but also the many other scales previously discussed that operate both across and independent from national scales. Additionally, these systems not only interact with other linguistic and cultural systems but also with each other and other related CAS such as communication and mode (Baker & Ishikawa, 2021). The interaction of culture and language as CAS in communication can be represented in Figure 1.

This relational and interactive stance matches well with previous claims of the need to look at each instance of communication to understand how culture and language come together. As the complexity theorist Gleick famously stated, 'the act of playing the game has a way of changing the rules' (1998: 24), so each instance of communication 'has a way of changing' how language and culture are connected.

2.3.5 Summary

In this section, we have considered four related perspectives on language and culture: linguistic relativity, the language-culture nexus, linguistic and cultural flows, and complexity theory. Linguistic relativity is probably the most well-known approach to understanding language and culture. It is also the most frequent approach in language teaching in which languages are strongly tied to

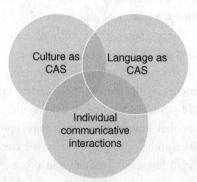

Figure 1 Language and culture as complex adaptive systems (adapted from Baker & Ishikawa, 2021)

particular national cultures (see Risager, 2007; Holliday, 2011; Baker, 2015a). However, it is important to stress that the strong version of this, in which languages and cultures are synonymous and all-encompassing in how we understand the world, is not supported by empirical evidence. More relevant is the weak version of linguistic relativity in which language influences our worldview but does not control it. Yet, even under this weak version, we need to be careful not to assume that particular languages are necessarily tied to particular cultures, especially at the national scale. Although language is never culturally neutral since it always has meaning for the individual and should be viewed as a cultural practice, it is not inexorably tied to any particular 'named' culture. Instead, the conceptualisations of languages and cultures under the language-culture nexus, linguistic and cultural flows, and complexity theory, all emphasise the fluid and dynamic links between language and culture. Following these perspectives, particular linguistic resources and cultural practices and references come together in a myriad of ways that can only be determined by examining each instance of communication.

In sum, throughout this first section the importance of viewing language as a cultural practice has been emphasised. This means that, when teaching and learning a language, culture will always be present whether or not it is explicitly recognised by teachers or learners. However, how language and culture come together is complex and not easy to predict a priori, suggesting that teaching culture may not be straightforward. This becomes even more complex when considering the use of second languages (L2) and multilingualism, which is the case for additional language learning and use. Moreover, languages learnt and used as an L2 are typically used across different cultural groupings in intercultural communication. How this takes places and how communicators make sense of this complexity will be the subject of the next section when we turn to intercultural and transcultural communication.

3 Intercultural and Transcultural Communication

3.1 Introduction

In the previous section we highlighted the close ties between language and culture and the importance of viewing them as interrelated (although not synonymous) for language learning. However, we also need to recognise that in L2/additional language learning and teaching, languages will be used in multilingual scenarios across cultural groupings. In other words, when learning and teaching an additional language, it is typically for multilingual intercultural communication. Like culture, intercultural communication is a broad term that is used in many different disciplines and has a multitude of definitions. Yet, at the same time, for many of us intercultural communication is ubiquitous. Globalisation has resulted in movements of large numbers of people across geographical and cultural borders with the result that many contemporary societies have a large variety of different languages and cultures present. Furthermore, telecommunications advances and particularly digital communication have given much of the world (but not all) the opportunity to interact instantly with anyone, anywhere. Even in societies where we do not find ourselves in regular physical contact with people who have different first languages and cultural identifications, we are still able to engage with a multitude of different cultures through global connections and especially the Internet. Thus, we are able to interact with and consume cultural practices and products from around the world, such as Hollywood movies, Thai food, Italian fashion and Chinese electronics. And, of course, the recent Covid-19 pandemic has illustrated just how globally connected even the most remote areas of the world are, as well as the continued importance of national borders.

In this section definitions of intercultural communication of relevance to applied linguistics and language teaching are outlined. It begins by contextualising intercultural communication research and distinguishing it from earlier cross-cultural communication studies. The importance of critical approaches to intercultural communication are emphasised. Similar to the previous discussion of culture, these eschew stereotyped and essentialist comparisons between national scale cultural and linguistic differences and, instead, explore the dynamic adaptability of languages and cultures in intercultural communication. Nonetheless, it is argued that intercultural communication research has not gone far enough in conceptualising the fluid links between languages and cultures in the complex communicative scenarios that are frequent in contemporary societies. Transcultural communication is proposed as an approach which builds on critical intercultural communication but is better able to account for the multitude of linguistic resources, cultural practices and scales that are simultaneously present in communication. Transcultural communication also links intercultural communication to current translanguaging and transmodality perspectives in applied linguistics and teaching. Again, as with the previous section, this discussion of theory is important in laying down a foundation for understanding the competences needed for successful intercultural and transcultural communication through an L2 and, in turn, better understanding how we might teach languages.

3.2 Understanding Intercultural Communication

A useful starting point in understanding intercultural communication research is to consider the history of the subject and how it has evolved. Piller proposes 'that discourses of culture, cultural difference and intercultural communication arose in the historical context of the nineteenth and twentieth centuries as part of the processes of colonialism' (2017: 14). Such research typically distinguished features of different cultures at the national level making use of essentialist stereotypes and 'othering'. The aim was frequently to establish the supposed 'superiority' and 'civilization' of colonising nations rather than to promote meaningful intercultural interaction – a useful reminder that issues of power and ideology have been present since the start of the field. In the twentieth century these ideas were taken up in cross-cultural communication research, which also focussed on national scale characterisations and comparisons of culture. Again the aim was often to provide advantages to particular nations and cultures, for example through Hall's (1959) work for the US military or Hofstede's (1980) research for IBM which promoted the communicative practices of North Americans and Europeans and particularly Anglophone English speakers. Thus, cross-cultural communication research involves the study of the communicative practices of distinct cultural groups independent from interactions (e.g. British communicative practices versus German communicative practices). Under this perspective, cultures are viewed as homogeneous, separable entities at the national scale, and a priori assumptions are made about people's cultural groupings and their influence on communication. While comparisons between cultures and nations have a role in intercultural communication research, the simplistic, stereotyped perspectives in cross-cultural communication approaches are more likely to hinder than help an understanding of what happens in intercultural interactions. As Piller notes, 'some of the research that has come to centrally define the field is certainly cringe inducing in the ways in which it reproduces essentialist discourses of culture rather than questions them' (2011: 172).

There are a number of fundamental differences between these earlier cross-cultural perspectives and more recent critical intercultural communication approaches. As highlighted by Scollon and Scollon (2001), the most important difference is that intercultural communication research focusses on the communicative practices of distinct cultural or other groups *in interaction* with each other. This is in contrast to the comparisons of communicative practices of national groups in cross-cultural communication. So, for example, while cross-cultural research compares the communicative practices of British and German people, intercultural communication research investigates what happens in the interaction between participants identified as German and British. Furthermore, in intercultural communication research, there is no a priori assumptions about how different groupings will influence the communication, and national scales are approached as one of many which can be drawn on in communication. Thus, groupings such as profession, gender, generation and ethnicity may prove as important (or more important) than nation in interpreting the interaction. Moreover, participants may draw on and construct emergent, adaptable and hybrid cultures which are not fixed to one particular nation but rather 'between' cultures. From an intercultural perspective, cultures are seen as heterogeneous, containing a great deal of variety among its members with boundaries that are fluid, dynamic and blurred. In other words, intercultural communication research adopts the semiotic, discourse, practice and ideological perspectives on culture outlined in Section 2.

Following this interactional perspective, Zhu defines intercultural communication research as 'primarily concerned with how individuals, in order to achieve their communication goals, negotiate cultural or linguistic differences which may be perceived relevant by at least one party in the interaction' (2019: 210). Additionally, cultural and linguistic differences may also be perceived as important by researchers, with the caveat that their relevance needs to be empirically or theoretically justified and not simply assumed (Baker, 2015a). From an intercultural perspective, these cultural and linguistic 'differences' are not seen as problems to be overcome, as in cross-cultural communication research, but rather as a range of variable resources that are made use of in interaction. Therefore, the focus is not on communicative problems but on how participants in intercultural communication successfully make use of these diverse resources to achieve their communicative goals. Nonetheless, despite the dynamic and practice orientated approaches in intercultural communication research, we need to maintain a critical attitude to the categorisations used. As Holliday (2011) points out, much intercultural communication research still falls into the trap of 'neo-essentialism'. Under neo-essentialism, cultures are understood as complex and made up of many different groups and identifications. However, this complexity takes place within the boundaries of the national culture which is regarded as the norm with other groupings viewed as 'sub-cultures'. In relation to intercultural communication, this foregrounding of the national results in an indelible 'intercultural line' (Holliday, 2011: 164) between 'our' culture and the 'foreign' other. This, in turn, can result in the same stereotyping and othering seen in cross-cultural communication research. We, therefore, need to continue to ask the questions proposed in relation to culture in Section 2, '[w]ho has introduced culture as a relevant category, for what purposes, and with what consequences?' (Scollon & Scollon, 2001: 545).

A number of core concepts have emerged which aid in critically explicating the relationship between individuals, communities and cultural systems: interculturality, third spaces, communities of practice and small cultures. Interculturality (e.g. Young & Sercombe, 2010; Zhu, 2019) explores how individuals make use of cultural memberships and identities in interaction, emphasising the constructed, emergent and negotiated nature of cultural identities. The importance of power and ideology are highlighted with identities both self-ascribed but also ascribed by others, especially in relation to issues of nationality, ethnicity and race (Zhu & Li, 2016; Zhu, 2019). The concept of third spaces (Kramsch, 1993) also focusses on the individual but is specifically concerned with L2 users who are seen as occupying a 'third space' that is neither part of an L1 culture or the 'target' L2 culture. L2 users operate on a 'cultural faultline' (Kramsch, 1993: 205) between cultures in which hybrid, dynamic and emergent cultural and linguistic practices are created. This approach has been very influential in applied linguistics and language teaching (and we will return to it in Sections 4 and 5 when discussing intercultural awareness and pedagogy); however, it has also been critiqued as potentially reifying and neo-essentialist in that participants in intercultural communication may not always be 'between' identifiable cultures or languages (Baker, 2015a; Holliday, 2011).

Moving away from the individual to the level of groups, communities of practice (CoP) (Lave and Wenger, 1991; Wenger, 1998) has been a useful framework for thinking about how communities are constructed at scales other than the national, and they are formed according to three criteria: mutual engagement, joint enterprise and shared repertoires (Wenger, 1998). We see CoP all around us in our everyday life through workplace, education, sporting and leisure groups, and their influence is easier to document than imagined national cultural groups, thus potentially avoiding simplification and stereotypes. However, CoP are limited in the types of groups they can account for. In many intercultural interactions, the relationships may be too brief to establish CoP; other groups, such as families and friends, may be more nebulous and less focussed than a CoP. At the same time, due to their small scale, CoP are not able to explain large scale cultural groupings, such as nations, ethnicities or religions where all participants do not regularly interact with each other or necessarily share goals and repertoires. Small cultures is an idea proposed by Holliday (1999; 2013) which, while similar to CoP in focussing on the local scale, is able to encompass more variable and less instrumental groupings such as families and friends, as well as temporary groups or communities such as those established in brief interactions. Small cultures are constructed through shared practices and discourses which build up over time. In the case of long-term small cultures, these conventions can become invisible. Moreover, these conventions give rise to a sense that the group is distinct from other groups. In researching small cultures, like interculturality approaches, it is important to focus on the interactions and how culture is constructed through them in order to avoid a priori essentialised cultural categories. Furthermore, small cultures are not viewed as a sub-culture within national cultures. The role of imagined national cultures is not denied, and it can be an important part of how small cultures are formed (Holliday, 2011). Nonetheless, small cultures help to understand the many different cultures and communities we belong to, the complex interaction between them, and the manner in which we may identify with and orientate toward different communities at different times in interactions.

3.2.1 Language and Intercultural Communication

In Section 2.3 we outlined the links between language and culture suggesting that language should be seen as a cultural practice but also that named languages and cultures (e.g. French language and French culture) were not synonymous. The language-culture nexus was put forward as a way to explain how languages and cultures are linked for individuals and in the most general sense, hence, meaning that language is never culturally neutral. Yet, at the same time, particular linguistic resources and cultural practices are not necessarily tied to any named culture or language at the national or other scale. Notions of transcultural flows and complexity theory were proposed to explain the dynamic and variable manner in which linguistic and other cultural resources and practices come together in each instance of communication. These ideas are equally relevant when considering the connections between languages and cultures in intercultural communication. This section explores the relationships between language and culture in specific relation to intercultural communication. Investigations into English use in intercultural communication will be drawn on as an extensive body of research has grown up in the last few decades on this, especially in the field of ELF (see Jenkins et al., 2018). However, apart from the scale at which English is used, there is nothing unique about English in intercultural communication and many of the ideas expressed here are applicable to other languages used in intercultural communication.

One of the most prominent features of language use in intercultural communication is that it is typically multilingual. Although there may be rare instances of intercultural communication where people share an L1 and no other languages are present (for instance monolingual English speakers from different cultures within the Anglophone world), in the vast majority of cases multilingualism is the norm. This multilingualism may be overt or covert (Cogo, 2018). Overt multilingualism refers to communication where two or more languages are clearly present in the discourse. The most obvious form of this is code-switching or mixing where participants change between different languages in the interaction. This may be done for a variety of reasons including: accommodating to their interlocutor when linguistic resources are shared (e.g. greeting in one language and then switching to another for the main discourse), making 'local' references when there is no obvious translation in the main language used (e.g. place names), to signal a speaker's L1 cultural identity, and to indicate a shared multilingual identity (e.g. exchanging words or phrases in the participants' L1s) (Cogo, 2018). Covert multilingualism refers to interactions which, on the surface, appear to be in one language but where the participants' various L1s influence the use of language. Covert multilingualism has been extensively documented in ELF research through features such as the use of idioms that mix metaphors from different L1s (e.g. Pitzl, 2018a) and original usage of words or word forms in English influenced by the L1. It is important to stress that the use of different languages and linguistic resources in intercultural communication are not viewed as strategies to make up for 'deficiencies' in another language. Rather they are viewed as proficient and creative uses of multilingual repertories and resources that are adapted to each instance of intercultural communication (Cogo, 2018).

Moving to identity, community and culture in intercultural communication, the role of language is equally dynamic and variable. Again drawing on ELF research, participants in ELF studies have reported and been observed using English, alongside other linguistic resources, to create and index multiple cultural resources, identities and groups. Research has explored how English and L1s are used in intercultural communication to move between 'local' and more 'global' orientations and 'shuttle' between communities (Canagarajah, 2007). English can function as a shared resource in the construction of and identification with dynamic communities of practice in business (Ehrenreich, 2009), academia (Kalocsai, 2014) and virtual spaces (Vettorel, 2014). English is frequently used in intercultural communication with other shared linguistic resources to create transient communities in more temporary interactions (e.g. Pitzl, 2018b). Studies have also shown the use of English in creating liminal, hybrid and third-place identities with participants embracing being 'in-between' and mediating between cultures or other groupings (e.g. Baker, 2009; 2011). Furthermore, as suggested in the previous paragraph, the multilingual and multicultural nature of the interactions may be a key shared feature in identification with dynamic, adaptable and transient communities in intercultural communication through ELF (Pitzl, 2018b). Nonetheless, as with all forms of communication, power and ideology are still important factors, and not all uses of English or other linguistic resources are necessarily regarded equally (Blommaert, 2010). This can result in different status assigned to different participants depending on both perceived proficiency in and varieties of

English used, as well as the value given to other languages used (e.g. Jenks, 2018).

Given this superdiversity (Blommaert, 2010) and complexity of languages and cultures in intercultural communication, traditional ways of thinking about these categories and the relationships between them become problematic. As highlighted throughout this Element, there are no fixed relationships between particular linguistic resources and cultural practices and references. Thus, a priori assumptions of a link between national scales of cultures and languages runs the risk of simplifying and essentialising interactions. However, at the same time, we need to be careful not to engage in neo-essentialism and assume that there are particular cultures or languages that participants in intercultural communication are 'between' (Holliday, 2013). Ideas such as third places, while useful in moving beyond the national scale, can still reify intercultural communication through assumptions about 'first' languages and cultures and 'target' languages and cultures (Baker, 2015a). The complexity of intercultural communication shown in ELF research indicates that it is not always clear what cultures or languages participants are in-between, with participants making use of multiple languages and scales simultaneously. Therefore, the 'inter' of *inter*cultural communication becomes problematic since participants are not necessarily in-between any one identifiable culture or language. New ways of thinking about languages and cultures in intercultural communication are needed.

3.3 Transcultural Communication

Just as data from intercultural interactions highlighted the limitations of cross-cultural approaches to understanding intercultural communication, so current research on intercultural communication, multilingualism and Global Englishes raises issues with intercultural communication perspectives (e.g. Baker, 2015a; Jenkins et al., 2018). As discussed in the previous section, the complexity and fluidity of linguistic and cultural resources and practices problematises the 'inter' metaphor in intercultural communication. Instead the 'trans' metaphor is a more appropriate one suggesting movement through, rather than in-between, and transcending and transgressing established norms and boundaries. Thus, replacing the 'inter' prefix with 'trans' transcultural communication can be characterised as:

> communication where interactants are seen moving through and across, rather than in-between, cultural and linguistic boundaries in which those very borders become blurred and transcended. Furthermore, boundary-crossing and blurring, whether as an unconscious part of everyday

communicative practices or as a deliberate transgressive act, highlights the transformative nature of such interactions whereby 'named' languages and cultures can no longer be taken for granted.

(Baker & Sangiamchit, 2019: 473)

Nonetheless, unlike the fundamental differences in perspective between cross-cultural and intercultural approaches, transcultural communication research builds on, rather than replaces, intercultural communication research. Furthermore, national scale cultures and languages are not ignored since they are a potentially powerful ideology that influences communication (Holliday, 2011). Similarly, hybridity, 'in-betweeness' and third places may still be relevant but we should not assume that they are necessarily so. Most significantly, transcultural perspectives are needed to adequately account for communication 'where participants transcend cultural and linguistic boundaries, rather than mix them, and crucially where the complexity of the interaction means boundaries themselves cannot easily be discerned' (Baker & Sangiamchit, 2019: 473). In transcultural communication these critical and dynamic perspectives on languages, cultures and their boundaries are the *starting point* of the investigation rather than the end point. At the same time it should be pointed out that the kinds of communication envisaged in transcultural communication are not exotic or unusual but very common in the multilingual and multicultural social groupings that many of us are part of.

Although the concept of transcultural communication as presented here is new, the notion of transculturality is not new. Pratt's (2008) highly influential transcultural theories have examined alternative post-colonial perspectives to language and culture. However, despite the use of the trans term, it is an approach nearer to third places with its focus on cultural adaptation and hybridity in contact zones. Closer to the approach taken here are Clifford's (1992) 'travelling' and 'translocal' cultures and Welsch's (1999) transculturality. Both Clifford and Welsch emphasise notions of culture that are dynamic and fluid with people seen as moving *through* cultural borders; however, neither is concerned with language in any detail and certainly not language teaching. Guilherme and Dietz (2015) offer a useful overview of the similarities and differences between conceptualisations of multicultural, intercultural and transcultural. While they observe that the diverse uses to which the terms have been put mean that 'it is impossible to establish fixed and stable lines between them' (2015: 1), they also argue that, given their importance in contemporary socio-cultural studies, we must attempt to be as precise as we can. Of most relevance to this discussion, Guilherme and Dietz underscore that from transcultural perspectives, multiple cultures and timescales are simultaneously present with no clear borders between them (2015: 8). Directly relevant to applied linguistics and language teaching perspectives are the concepts of transcultural flows (discussed in Section 2), particularly Risager's (2006) transnational flows and Pennycook's (2007) transcultural flows. Additionally, Canagarajah's (2013) exploration of translingual practices makes use of the scale metaphor to 'unpack' the multiple overlapping layers of context that are simultaneously brought together in translingual spaces. Importantly, for Canagarajah scales are not predetermined but open and negotiated where 'the layered simultaneity of scales and norms in any given place is unpacked and renegotiated to construct translocal spaces' (2013: 172). Throughout this Element, we will make use of the notion of transcultural flows and scales to explore the links between languages and cultures in contemporary social spaces, as well as the implications for teaching language and culture.

In sum, we can view transcultural communication research as:

- The study of communicative practices where cultural and linguistic differences are relevant to participants or researchers but not necessarily linked to any particular group
- Cultures are seen as heterogeneous and cultural characterisations are contestable
- National cultures are one of many scales, ranging from the local to the global, and participants can move through and across scales rather than in-between
- Multiple scales can be simultaneously present in interactions
- Cultural practices and representations can be constructed in situ and emergent; participants are not necessarily in-between any named cultures
- Cultural and linguistic boundaries can be transcended and transgressed

(adapted from Baker & Ishikawa, 2021)

3.3.1 Language and Transcultural Communication

In the same way that intercultural communication research was linked to contemporary theories of multilingualism, so transcultural communication draws on current approaches to translanguaging. Similar to the manner in which cultural borders are transcended in transcultural communication, translanguaging theories explore 'the fluid and dynamic practices that transcend the boundaries between named languages, language varieties, and language and other semiotic systems' (Li, 2018: 9). Furthermore, Li proposes that the '[T]ranslanguaging Instinct drives humans to go beyond narrowly defined linguistic cues and transcend culturally defined language boundaries to achieve effective communication' (2018: 24–5). In other words, both transcultural communication and translanguaging examine how participants transcend, transgress and transform linguistic and cultural boundaries through their communicative practices. Again, such perspectives underscore the importance of eschewing a priori assumptions about the links between cultural and linguistic resources and the necessity of investigating the relationships as they are constructed in interactions.

Both transcultural communication and translanguaging can be viewed as part of the more general 'trans' turn in applied linguistics (Hawkins & Mori, 2018). Here too the trans prefix is used to highlight the importance of questioning boundaries between languages, modes, cultures and nations and to emphasise a more holistic approach to understanding communication and meaning making that does not artificially isolate and separate interrelated elements. However, as Hawkins and Mori explain, notions of transcending borders contain a contradiction or tension within them: 'these terms with the "trans-" prefix at once advocate for the appreciation of fluidity and flexibility seen in contemporary society and underscore the very existence of categories, borders, and boundaries that are called into question '(2018: 1). To put it more simply, in order to transcend a border, there must be a border to transcend. Therefore, we need to recognise the power of the ideological categories of languages and cultures, especially at national scales, 'while simultaneously attempting to critically engage with the power structures that naming creates' (Baker & Sangiamchit, 2019: 471). These two perspectives on language and communication are succinctly summed up by Garcia and Kleyn who underscore the social and political power of named languages but also their limitations in explaining actual communicative practices: 'for us, translanguaging refers to the deployment of a speaker's full linguistic repertoire, which does not in any way correspond to the socially and politically defined boundaries of named languages' (2016: 14).

A core aspect of translanguaging is viewing communication as more than the use of just the linguistic resources that have traditionally been the focus of research and, instead, considering all the semiotic resources employed in meaning making (Hawkins & Mori, 2018; Li, 2018). As Pennycook observes, 'the separation of language from the complexity of signs with which its use is associated has limited our understanding of a broader semiotics' (2007: 49). Multimodal theories and research have been central in understanding the range of modes utilised in communication, such as gestures, images, writing, layout and music (e.g. Kress & van Leeuwen, 2001; Kress, 2017). From multimodal theories, transmodality has been developed to describe the *processes* by which a range of modes are used simultaneously with boundaries between modes blurring and indistinct (e.g. Sultana, 2016; Hawkins, 2018; Baker & Sangiamchit, 2019). Newfield refers to this as 'the transmodal moment' (2017: 103) where meaning and affect are created through the interaction of a range of modes simultaneously and where attempts to isolate modes would lose a holistic understanding of the interaction.

Research into the use of English as a global language and particularly ELF has been concerned with many of the same issues as transcultural and translanguaging perspectives. This includes an interest in English as part of a multilingual repertoire and fluid, liminal cultural practices, identities and groupings that are not linked to any one language or culture (e.g. Baker, 2015a; Baker & Ishikawa, 2021). For example, in proposing that English should be understood as a multilingua franca (EMF), Jenkins writes that it is 'used predominantly in transcultural communication among multilingual English speakers, who will make use of their full linguistic repertoires as appropriate in the context of any specific interaction' (2018: 601). Research in this area is new, but there are a growing number of conceptual (e.g. Baker, 2018; Baker & Ishikawa, 2021; Jenkins, 2015; 2018; Pitzl, 2018b) and empirical studies (e.g. Baker & Sangiamchit, 2019; Cogo, 2016; Dovchin et al., 2016; Ishikawa, 2020; Sultana, 2016) which have taken up trans- perspectives on ELF. Li (2016) presents one the first studies of ELF that combined a translingual and transmodal approach through analyses of 'Chinglish' in advertising, public signs and various online domains. Figure 2 illustrates the transmodal possibilities of translanguaging through the combination of the text 'I', the heart symbol and the Chinese flag to produce the phrase 'I love China'.

Importantly, and following the argument made here in support of transcultural communication, Li proposes that we need to go beyond notions such as hybridity to account for the complexity of these communicative practices (2016: 20).

Figure 2 A translanguaging sign (Li Wei, 2016: 6)

Similarly, other ELF research has looked at how languages, modes and cultural practices and references combine in complex ways through processes of transcultural communication, translanguaging and transmodality to produce meaning and affect. In the following example from Baker and Sangiamchit (2019), two international students in the UK are engaged in playful teasing on the popular SNS (social networking site) Facebook. Ken (L1 Thai, male) posts an edited photo and text (figure 3) combining an image of martial arts film star Jet Li with text from another martial arts film star Bruce Lee on his friend Hessam's (L1 Farsi, male) Facebook wall. This is done, as Ken explains in an interview, to tease Hessam, as Hessam is a fan of Jet Li but dislikes Bruce Lee.

Extract 3.1 Jet Lee

Figure 3 Jet Lee

Ken to Hessam
01 Ken: Hope you like it. Good night...
Like · Share · 9 hours ago
SM likes this.
02 Hessam: you are a bastard Ken! I am gone kill you! :)
9 hours ago · Like · 1
03 Ken: You are very welcome;)
9 hours ago · Like · 1
04 Hessam: the family name is also need correction! it
05   should read 'Li' instead of 'Lee'
9 hours ago · Like
06 Ken: OK Thanks That's gonna be the next version
9 hours ago · Like · 1
07 Hessam: bastard! I really like this guy! and he was the true champion

08		of china from the age of 11 to 19 for 8 consecutive years winning gold
09		medals! now you are making joke with him … I am gone show you the
10		cannon feast punch tomorrow!
9 hours ago · Like · 1		
11	Hessam:	just kidding of course! no need to move away
12		from Southampton mate!
9 hours ago · Like · 1		

(Baker & Sangiamchit, 2019: 482)

The exchange begins with a use of multimodal resources through the image of Jet Li next to text and some deliberate editing of the text in which the evidence of the change is left explicit. The language use on the surface appears to be in English, but rather than any particular variety of English, it has variable uses of ELF with the 'covert' multilingualism that underpins this. Moreover, the discussion of the spelling of Jet Li's surname in lines 4–6 is not straightforwardly attributable to any one language: it could be English, Cantonese or Putonghua. Likewise, the phrase 'canon feast punch' (line 10) is not easily assigned to any particular named language. A translanguaging perspective is more appropriate in which these are seen as resources from the participants' multilingual repertoires. Additionally, emoticons (lines 2 & 3) and punctuation (lines 10 & 12) are used to add further affect to the exchange. Thus, the multimodal resources of images, text and emoticons combine through transmodal processes to construct the humorous and friendly nature of this interaction. Turning to the cultural dimensions, we see multiple cultural scales simultaneously present. There are the two martial arts film stars (Jet Li and Bruce Lee) who are globally recognised but also associated with China and Hong Kong. Martial arts is also globally familiar but historically linked to China and East Asia. There are references to local geographical places familiar to the participants (Southampton, line 12). However, the inter-action itself takes place in the virtual space of an SNS. In sum, in this example we can see the manner in which multiple resources, linguistic and multimodal, come together in variable ways and are used to construct and represent various cultural scales and practices simultaneously. It is also worth noting that at no point in this exchange are the participants' L1s or 'national cultures' made salient to the interaction.

3.4 Summary

We began by underscoring that L2 or additional language use is almost always intercultural in one way or another, and so understanding intercultural communication in language learning and teaching is important. Intercultural communication was distinguished from earlier more essentialist cross-cultural approaches that compared cultures at national scales. In intercultural communication research, the focus is on interactions between participants from different linguistic and cultural backgrounds when those differences become relevant to the communication. Intercultural communication was characterised as multilingual and multicultural with hybridity and third places as core aspects. However, we also needed to be careful not to reify language and culture in intercultural communication and make assumptions about identifiable cultures and languages that participants are 'between'. Contemporary research in areas such as ELF and translanguaging has highlighted the complexity of linguistic, cultural and other semiotic resources in communication which cannot easily be attributed to named languages and cultures, especially at the national scale. Transcultural communication was proposed as a perspective that emphasised communication through, rather than between, cultural and linguistic borders, in which the borders themselves are transcended and transformed in the process. Transcultural communication was linked to commensurable theories of translanguaging and transmodality, which combined, provide a holistic picture of communication encompassing a range of semiotic resources and multiple cultural scales beyond named languages and cultures.

If the aim of language teaching is to prepare learners to communicate through the language they are learning (as opposed to just passing an exam or completing an academic course), then this communication will be intercultural and transcultural and will involve a much wider range of knowledge and skills than traditionally covered in pedagogy. Processes of intercultural and transcultural communication are as important as the 'language' used in communication. Furthermore, communication is likely to draw on variable, multilingual and multimodal resources through translanguaging and transmodal processes. How we might conceive of this expanded range of knowledge and skills for communication will be the topic of the next section.

4 Intercultural and Transcultural Awareness

4.1 Introduction

In Sections 2 and 3 we explored the links between language and culture in intercultural communication. The close connections between them were emphasised with language viewed as a cultural practice. This means that learning and using a language will always have a cultural dimension which should be recognised in teaching. However, it was also stressed that named languages and cultures are not necessarily tied (e.g. the 'English' language and 'British' culture). Instead, linguistic and other cultural practices and references come together in variable ways dependent on each interaction. Furthermore, we also looked at how use of an additional language (L2) was typically for intercultural communication across linguistic and cultural borders, meaning that the processes of learning and teaching an L2 are necessarily intercultural. Again the need to avoid oversimplification and essentialism was underscored, with linguistic and cultural differences and boundaries approached as fluid and negotiable. Transcultural communication was introduced as a contemporary perspective that focussed on communication *through* cultural and linguistic borders where the boundaries themselves are transgressed, transcended and transformed in the process.

Perspectives such as critical intercultural communication and transcultural communication suggest a more complex view of communication than that usually taken in applied linguistics and language teaching. This also means that the knowledge, skills and attitudes (i.e. competence) needed to successfully undertake such communication will need a similar increase in range to meet this complexity. As previously discussed in intercultural and transcultural approaches, communication involves more than just linguistic forms. Pragmatics, communication strategies, multimodality, linguistic and intercultural awareness are all key. Moreover, language is also approached differently with multilingualism being central, as well as with flexible approaches to linguistic forms and notions such as translanguaging becoming increasingly prominent. All of this has profound implications for language teaching. If the aim of language teaching is to enable learners to successfully communicate through the language they are learning, then equipping them with the necessary competence is crucial. Within applied linguistics and language teaching this has frequently been dealt with under the topic of communicative competence. Yet, as repeatedly stressed in this Element, L2 learners are engaged in intercultural and transcultural communication and so need *intercultural* and *transcultural* communicative competence. In this section we critically evaluate communicative competence as it has been conceived in language teaching and suggest intercultural communicative competence as a more appropriate and comprehensive notion. Nonetheless, there are also a number of limitations to intercultural communicative competence and so we go on to examine contemporary research and theory regarding the knowledge, skills and attitudes necessary to successfully engage in transcultural communication. Intercultural and transcultural awareness is proposed as an especially relevant approach.

4.2 Communicative Competence

Although a detailed review of communicative competence is neither feasible nor appropriate for this Element, it is important to outline some of its key tenets since they have been so influential in language teaching and inform later approaches discussed here. Hymes' concept (1972) of communicative competence for first language (L1) users and its subsequent adaptation for L2 users by Canale and Swain (1980) have been foundational in applied linguistics and language teaching. Hymes' competence contains four aspects: whether something is formally possible, feasible, appropriate and actually performed (1972: 281). Importantly, under Hymes' conceptualisation the sociolinguistic aspects of communication (appropriateness and actually performed) are as crucial as the linguistic (formally possible). Moreover, Hymes viewed communicative competence as a form of cultural knowledge and proposed that 'between the linguistic and the cultural; certainly the spheres of the two will interact' (1972: 286). Nonetheless, Hymes was focussed on L1 native speakers of a language and relatively homogeneous speech communities, neither of which are appropriate for L2 users and intercultural communication. Canale and Swain (1980) drew extensively on Hymes but focussed on L2 learners with a model of communicative competence that involved grammatical, sociolinguistic and strategic competence, with discourse competence later added (Canale, 1983). Yet, despite the focus on L2 learners, the model of a successful communicator was still the inappropriate native speaker and this is what L2 users were expected to conform to, both grammatically and sociolinguistically. Moreover, as Byram (2021: 13–14) notes, while Canale and Swain maintained Hymes' sociolinguistic elements, they did not include the sociocultural aspects. Additionally, in language teaching the linguistic/grammatical elements of communicative competence have been foregrounded at the expense of the sociolinguistic, which are typically dealt with in a superficial and narrow manner (Leung, 2005; Hall, 2013). Lastly, both Hymes and Canale and Swain have been critiqued for adopting an overly static view of language and communication that does not pay sufficient attention to the agency of users and their adaptation and negotiation of linguistic and other communicative resources and practices (e.g. Brumfit, 2001; Widdowson, 2012).

More recent discussions of communicative competence have addressed some of these limitations, particularly concerning the focus on native speakers and static approaches to language. Cook's multi-competence is defined as 'knowledge of more than one language in the same mind' (2002: 10) and positions multilingualism at the centre of the model. Cook adds that for L2 users the monolingual native speaker is irrelevant since it is competence in *languages* rather than a language that is crucial (2008). Hall (2013) takes this approach a step further in proposing that competence will not be in discrete languages but rather in plurilithic individual linguistic resources which do not necessarily correspond to named languages. A similar idea is proposed by Blommaert (2010) who argues that we should not think of competence in specific languages but rather as linguistic resources and repertories that enable us to engage in communicative practices. Blommaert and Seidlhofer both suggest that, due to the inherent variability of languages used in multilingual scenarios, competence will not be fixed but instead always 'partial and incomplete' (Seidlhofer, 2011: 80) since we cannot have knowledge of the linguistics resources needed for every communicative context we find ourselves in. Moreover, Seidlhofer (2011) and Widdowson (2012), in relation to communication through ELF, argue that Hymes' notions of appropriateness and feasibility will be adaptable and variable, depending on negotiation in participants' particular communicative contexts. Importantly, such judgements are unlikely to be the same as or even made in reference to 'native-speaker' conventions. Widdowson (2012) goes on to add communicative and pragmatic strategies as equally, if not more, important in understanding communicative competence (a point returned to in Section 4.4).

4.3 Intercultural Communicative Competence

An approach to understanding the competencies needed for L2 users that explicitly and comprehensively incorporates the intercultural dimension is intercultural communicative competence. While there are various models of intercultural competence (see Spitzberg and Changnon (2009) for a discussion of over 200 models), as with communicative competence, the aim here is not to provide a comprehensive overview but instead focus on the elements that are of most relevance to this discussion. As such, the focus will be on Byram's (1997; 2008; 2021) intercultural communicative competence (ICC) model since it includes both communicative and intercultural competence, has been the most influential within language teaching, and informs many of the later models of competence/awareness explored in this Element. Byram (1997) begins with van Ek's (1986) language-based model which, similar to Canale and Swain (1980), comprises linguistic, sociolinguistic and discourse competence. To this are added Byram's own five elements (the five *savoirs*) of intercultural competence: attitudes (*savoir être*); knowledge (*savoirs*); skills of interpreting and relating (*savoir comprendre*); skills of discovery and interaction (*savoir apprendre/faire*); and critical cultural awareness/political education (*savoir s'engager*) (2021: 62–7). The central element is critical cultural awareness/political education which is defined as, '[a]n ability to evaluate, critically and on the basis of an explicit, systematic process of reasoning, values present in one's own and other cultures and countries' (2021: 66). In addition to going beyond linguistic competence in outlining the knowledge, skills and attitudes needed to engage in successful intercultural communication, Byram adds the intercultural speaker as the embodiment and target of ICC. Byram argues that this intercultural speaker is an 'attainable idea' as opposed to the inappropriate and unattainable 'native speaker' (2021: 96).

One important caveat to add when discussing ICC, and one which Byram (2021) repeatedly underscores, is that ICC is an educational model. In other words, the elements of ICC are proposed as knowledge, skills and attitudes which can be developed through education to equip learners of foreign languages to engage in intercultural communication through that language. What ICC is not is a model of what happens in intercultural communication and the competencies that may or may not be employed. This is an important distinction and Byram makes no claims to have based the elements of ICC on empirical data from intercultural communication. This is clearly a limitation of the model and, as seen when discussing transcultural communication (e.g. Baker, 2011; Baker & Sangiamchit, 2019), means ICC is not able to account for everything observed from actual instances of intercultural and transcultural communication. However, ICC's educational focus is also one of its strengths and it has been proven to be a very important and useful model in language education contexts. Therefore, ICC will be returned to in Section 5 when considering language teaching in more detail. Additionally, despite not being based on empirical data, many of the elements of ICC have been observed in research into intercultural interactions (e.g. Baker, 2011).

Another caveat which needs further explanation is Byram's use of country and nation as the main scale in discussing intercultural communication. Sections 2 and 3 made it clear that while nation is an important category in understanding intercultural and transcultural communication, it is one of many and we need to be careful to avoid assuming its relevance. The original formulation of ICC has been criticised as neo-essentialist in foregrounding and making assumptions about the links between culture, language, country and nation (Holliday, 2011; Baker, 2011; Baker, 2015a). In a revised model of ICC, Byram (2021: 11) stresses that country is used as a convenient term and does not refer to a single group or scale. Countries are approached as multilingual, multicultural and containing many communities (Byram, 2021: 1). Byram also suggests that the ICC model can be used to refer to communication between communities and cultures beyond the national scale but that country and nation are used both as a convenient shorthand to avoid detailed explanation and also because country and nation are typically the focus of education systems (Byram, 2021: 38).

Yet, even with these caveats the prominence given to country is still questionable. Country is not necessarily the most relevant scale in much transcultural communication and may not even feature at all as the examples in Sections 1 and 3 illustrated. Nonetheless, as Byram (2021) argues, we can still make use of ICC by replacing the term country with other relevant communities and cultural groupings in intercultural communication, but this is not a direction pursued by Byram himself. Furthermore, the use of the term 'foreign' is also problematic. For instance, in the case of English as a lingua franca it is nobody's L1 but equally not 'foreign' to anyone. Byram (2021: 153) acknowledges this and has helpfully removed some of the earlier simplistic understanding of ELF (Byram, 1997: 112) but has little to say about how this may influence ICC. Additionally, as the world's most learnt and used L2, English cannot easily be ignored in a language educational model. Furthermore, the claim that intercultural interactions need to be understood as in one way or another involving a 'host' and a 'visitor' would suggest that the implications of globalisation on communities and languages has not been fully incorporated into ICC (Byram, 2021: 43). In many intercultural and transcultural interactions, for example at an international conference, in a multinational corporation, an international university or a virtual community, the distinction between a host and visitor is of questionable relevance. Other ways of thinking about communities and their participants are needed such as communities of practice, transient international communities, small cultures, translanguaging and virtual spaces (e.g. Baker & Sangiamchit, 2019; Ehrenreich, 2018; Holliday, 2013; Li, 2018; Pitzl, 2018b). These dynamic conceptions of community are as relevant to any language, not only English, used in intercultural communication in multilingual and multicultural scenarios.

We might also want to question the links between language and culture in ICC given that it makes use of a model of communicative competence that is very similar to the already criticised model from Canale and Swain (1980). This is a limitation Byram is aware of, and he has reformulated linguistic, sociolinguistic and discourse competence in an updated version of ICC to make it clear that they are related to competencies of an intercultural speaker, not a native speaker, with meanings and conventions negotiable (Byram, 2021: 60–1). However, linguistic competence is still related to knowledge of 'the rules of a standard version of the language' (2021: 60), which is problematic. How 'standard' is defined and made use of in teaching is neither straightforward nor uncontroversial and needs further thought. While knowledge of a standard variety of a language may be important, as ELF research has documented on numerous occasions, it is frequently not in itself sufficient in use or necessarily desirable as the goal in education (see Seidlhofer, 2018; Baker & Ishikawa, 2021). Other models of competence and awareness for intercultural communication that take a different approach to 'standardised' linguistic knowledge are considered later.

Overall, despite these limitations, ICC has proven to be key in understanding many of the knowledge, skills and attitudes of relevance to language education whose aim is to equip learners for intercultural communication. It has expanded communicative competence considerably and added substantial elements that address the intercultural dimensions of learning and using an L2. In ICC's most recent reformulation, Byram (2021) has also addressed some of the concerns around neo-essentialism and static approaches to language. However, it is still questionable how relevant this model is for transcultural communication when clear linguistic and cultural boundaries are not easy to establish and where national scales (no matter how complex and diverse) are less relevant. This may be more a matter of focus, and we cannot expect one model to cover all contexts; nonetheless, it suggests that alternative models of intercultural communicative competence and awareness are needed to both account for transcultural communication and to prepare learners for such scenarios.

4.4 Critical Approaches to Communicative and Intercultural Communicative Competence

Again the aim of this section is to provide a focussed discussion, rather than a full overview, of a number of relevant models of the competence and awareness needed by learners and users of an L2 for intercultural and transcultural communication. Canagarajah's performative competence builds explicitly on Byram's ICC in its focus on processes (performance) of intercultural communication and the wide range of knowledge, skills and attitudes employed (2013: 173). However, Canagarajah envisages a different notion of community to that taken by Byram, drawing on Pratt's (2008) idea of contact zones to explore translingual communication, fluid cultural groupings and their power relationships. This is underpinned by the use of a scale metaphor to account for the multiple scales and intersecting orders of indexicality and polycentricity in which these contact zones become translocal spaces. In performative competence, competence is not of a fixed abstract mental representation of language but 'competence for plural language norms and mobile semiotic resources' (2013: 173). Canagarajah goes on to explain that 'translinguals have the ability to align diverse semiotic resources to create meaning and achieve communicative success when words in isolation are inadequate and homogeneous norms are not available in contact zones' (2013: 174). Such competence involves communicative and pragmatic strategies for the micro-management of specific interactions embedded in more general social and linguistic awareness and supported by cooperative disposi- tions. However, Canagarajah stresses that, due to the performative nature of competence, none of these competencies are fixed and so should not be conceived or taught as a single 'best' approach to communication (2013: 186).

Kramsch's (2009; 2011) concept of symbolic competence is also based on a more critical view of culture than the perspectives in ICC. Kramsch is focussed on the symbolic dimensions to the intercultural, not as a component in a set of competencies for intercultural communication, but as a mindset or mentality for engaging in multilingual and multicultural communication. Thus, symbolic com- petence is a flexible and holistic combination of knowledge, experience and judgement rather than the more stable knowledge and competencies of ICC (Byram, 2021: 70). Kramsch makes use of a discourse approach to culture in which symbolic competence is about understanding the complexity of multiple 'discourse worlds' (2011: 356) with a diversity of meanings and interpretations of culture and communication. Equally important is reflexivity on the ideological, historic and aesthetic aspects of intercultural communication and their relation- ship to L2 language learning and teaching (2009: 199). Core aspects of symbolic competence are:

- an ability to understand the symbolic value of symbolic forms and the different cultural memories evoked by different symbol systems
- an ability to draw on the semiotic diversity afforded by multiple languages to reframe ways of seeing familiar events, create alternative realities, and find an appropriate subject position 'between languages', so to speak
- an ability to look both at and through language and to understand the challenges to the autonomy and integrity of the subject that come from unitary ideologies and a totalizing networked culture.

(Kramsch 2009: 201)

Multilingualism is fundamental to symbolic competence, including an awareness of the forms of languages but also the ability to look 'at and through' them. The critical dimension is also explicit in the challenges to 'unitary ideologies and totalizing networked culture'. Furthermore, sym- bolic competence represents a refinement of the notion of third places in Kramsch's (1993) earlier writing. As Kramsch argues, 'the notion of third culture must be seen less as a PLACE than as a symbolic PROCESS of meaning-making that sees beyond the dualities of national languages (L1–L2) and national cultures (C1–C2)' (2011: 355). Finally, as made clear in the previous quotation, symbolic competence, like performative competence, is viewed from a performative and process perspective in which it is a 'dynamic, flexible, and locally contingent competence' (2009: 199).

Within the field of Global Englishes, and particularly ELF research, there has been considerable research and theorisation on the competences utilised in successful intercultural communication through English (much of which is equally relevant to any language used in intercultural and transcultural communication). These have typically focussed on flexible use of language alongside communicative and pragmatic strategies. Indeed, it was noted early in ELF research that, despite the anticipated communication problems due to linguistic and cultural differences, the observed interactions were typically successful (e.g. Jenkins, 2000). This was attributed to the predominantly cooperative disposition of participants and extensive accommodation through the use of communicative and pragmatic strategies (Jenkins, 2000; Jenkins et al., 2011). This has led Seidlhofer and Widdowson to suggest that, rather than any particular use of language, 'it may turn out that what is distinctive about ELF lies in the communicative strategies that its speakers use' (2009: 37–8); although it seems likely that such communicative strategies will be part of any multilingual interactional interaction, rather than unique to ELF. Observed strategies have included accommodation through pronunciation and language adjustments, creative use of language to fit the context and participants (such as original word, phrase and idiom coinage), clarification, self-repair, repetition, reformulation, translation, code-switching and most recently translanguaging (Cogo & Pitzl, 2016; Jenkins et al., 2011; Jenkins et al., 2018; Seidlhofer, 2011). However, as with all intercultural communication, power imbalances and different ideologies have also been observed, especially as regards the status of 'native' and 'non-native' users of English (Jenkins, 2007; Seidlhofer, 2018) and also in less cooperative and more unequal ELF interactions (Jenks, 2018).

Current ELF research has emphasised the multilingual nature of all ELF communication through the concept of English as a multilingua franca (EMF), placing ELF within wider multilingual practices (Jenkins, 2015). This perspective is commensurable with the transcultural communication, translanguaging and transmodal approach taken in this Element, as Jenkins writes, EMF is 'used predominantly in transcultural communication among multilingual English speakers, who will make use of their full linguistic repertoires as appropriate in the context of any specific interaction' (2018: 601). Taking up this point Ishikawa (2021) and Baker and Ishikawa (2021) propose that accommodation will also need to be expanded beyond linguistic resources to transcultural and transmodal accommodation. Ishikawa (2020; 2021) goes on to outline the notion of EMF awareness, with awareness adopted in a broad sense as an alternative to competence (to be explained in detail in the following section).

> EMF awareness does not only aim to raise students' awareness (in a narrow sense) of the roles and effects of language and culture in communication and nurture confidence as English users. It also aims to enable students to connect this conscious understanding to their own transcultural and transmodal communication by appropriating English and multilingual resources in a flexible, situationally appropriate manner. (Baker & Ishikawa, 2021: 255)

Like ICC, EMF awareness is predominantly developed in response to educational needs, and similar to performative and symbolic competence, there is a focus on 'communicative *processes* rather than linguistic or other *products'* (Baker & Ishikawa, 2021: 256). In sum, these critical approaches to communicative and intercultural communicative competence such as EMF awareness, performative competence and symbolic competence, all adopt fluid perspectives on the connections between linguistic resources and cultural practices and references and so align well with transcultural communication.

4.5 Intercultural and Transcultural Awareness

In this final section, intercultural awareness (ICA) is outlined in detail as an approach that incorporates both ICC and critical perspectives on communicative and intercultural communicative competence. Furthermore, ICA is specifically attuned to the needs of language users and learners who are expected to engage in transcultural communication. Baker defines ICA as 'a conscious understanding of the role culturally based forms, practices and frames of reference can have in intercultural communication, and an ability to put these conceptions into practice in a flexible and context specific manner in communication' (Baker, 2015a: 163). Intercultural, rather than cultural, awareness is chosen to emphasise that the focus is on the processes of *inter*cultural communication rather than on understanding particular 'other' cultures and languages. Thus, in ICA, culture is not linked to countries or nationalities, nor does it assume an 'our/other' culture distinction. Transcultural awareness is perhaps a more appropriate term, particularly when referring to the more 'advanced' elements of ICA and has been added to these levels. Nonetheless, due to the more prevalent use of the term intercultural at the time the model was initially developed (Baker, 2009; 2011), and to link it to the wider research field, the term intercultural has still been retained. 'Awareness' serves as an alternative to the problematic competence/performance distinction (see Blommaert, 2010; Halliday, 1979; Harris, 1998; Pennycook, 2007). It is used in a broader holistic sense to refer to knowledge, skills, behaviour and attitudes and seeks to integrate cognition, attitudes and actual communicative practices (Baker & Ishikawa, 2021). This also serves to underscore that ICA is seen as a process rather than a fixed set of knowledge or behaviours. As emphasised in the second part of the definition, flexibility and adaptability in relation to emergent, situated communicative practices is crucial. Therefore, ICA serves as both a model of the elements of intercultural and transcultural communication based on empirical research and as a potential model for incorporating intercultural and transcultural communication into language teaching, with the caveat that, as with all models, it is a necessary simplification and abstraction of both (Baker, 2009; 2011; 2015a). It should also be noted that ICA was developed specifically in relation to the use of ELF scenarios (Baker, 2011); however, there is nothing inherent in the model which means it would not be applicable to other languages used in similarly multilingual, intercultural and transcultural communication interactions.

More detail of what ICA entails is given in the three levels and twelve components of ICA as outlined in Figure 4. The levels progress from essentialist 'basic' cultural awareness, to a more in-depth 'advanced' awareness of the complexity of culture and communication within and between different cultures, and finally to intercultural and transcultural awareness. Intercultural and transcultural awareness is the most complex and dynamic perspective and corresponds with the previously given definition of ICA, as well as being well-suited to transcultural communication. However, it is important to stress that this model does not propose that learners will necessarily develop and progress smoothly through the three levels. Some may never progress beyond basic or advanced cultural awareness, others may begin with intercultural/transcultural awareness (if, for example, they are brought up in a multicultural and multilingual environment and/or have extensive experience of transcultural communication). Furthermore, individuals may display different elements of the model in a non-linear manner indicating intercultural awareness at times, but at other times reverting to basic and essentialist cultural comparisons associated with level 1.

Level 1, basic cultural awareness, involves a somewhat simplistic and essentialist understanding of culture and communication, typically associated solely with the national scale. Awareness is displayed through generalised and possibly stereotyped comparisons between 'our' and 'other' cultures of a cross-cultural nature with little understanding of intercultural communication. Given how widespread such essentialist understanding of culture and communication is, it is important that any model of intercultural and transcultural communication is able to account for them, even if we may wish to move beyond them.

Level 1: basic cultural awareness

An awareness of:
1. culture as a set of shared behaviours, beliefs, and values;
2. the role culture and context play in any interpretation of meaning;
3. our own culturally based behaviour, values, and beliefs and the ability to articulate this;
4. others' culturally based behaviour, values, and beliefs and the ability to compare this with our own culturally based behaviour, values, and beliefs.

Level 2: advanced cultural awareness

An awareness of:
5. the relative nature of cultural norms;
6. cultural understanding as provisional and open to revision;
7. multiple voices or perspectives within any cultural grouping;
8. individuals as members of many social groupings including cultural ones;
9. common ground between specific cultures as well as an awareness of possibilities for mismatch and miscommunication between specific cultures.

Level 3: intercultural/transcultural awareness

An awareness of:
10. culturally based frames of reference, forms, and communicative practices as being related both to specific cultures and also as emergent and hybrid in intercultural communication;
11. initial interaction in intercultural communication as possibly based on cultural stereotypes or generalizations but an ability to move beyond these through:
12. a capacity to negotiate and mediate between different emergent communicative practices and frames of reference based on the above understanding of culture in intercultural communication.

Figure 4 The twelve components of intercultural awareness (adapted from Baker, 2015a: 164).

Level 2, advanced cultural awareness, incorporates more complex understandings of culture and communication. Cultures may be seen as diverse and made up of different groupings with multiple voices. There may also be experience of and detailed knowledge of 'other' cultures leading to an understanding of different communicative practices and the relative nature of cultural norms. Level 2 is therefore analogous to ICC (Byram, 1997; 2021) and third places (Kramsch, 1993), but like both of those perspectives, retains notions of an 'intercultural line' (Holliday, 2011) that separates cultures, with L2 users positioned between identifiable 'home' and 'target' cultures and languages. The national scale may also still be primary with other cultural groupings viewed as 'within' or 'between' national cultures.

At level 3, intercultural and transcultural awareness moves beyond the intercultural line and an 'our/other' culture dichotomy and instead, 'involves an awareness of cultures, languages and communication which are not correlated and tied to any single native speaker community or even group of communities' (Baker, 2015a: 166). Participants are able to move through multiple cultural scales simultaneously from the local to the national and the global, without necessarily being 'in-between' or hybridising any fixed cultural groupings or their communicative practices. Thus, the relationships between linguistic and other communicative resources and cultural practices are seen as dynamic, liminal and emergent. The ability to move beyond fixed generalisations and negotiate and adapt to these emergent communicative practices and cultural references in situ during intercultural and transcultural communication becomes core. Clearly the knowledge, skills and attitudes described at level 3 match the characteristics of transcultural communication outlined so far. While it may be unhelpful from the perspective of continuity to change the terminology of ICA, level 3 could accurately be referred to as transcultural awareness. In other words, it encompasses the awareness, in the broader sense of the term, needed to successfully engage in transcultural communication.

Extensive reference to language competence or awareness is not made in ICA; instead ICA refers to communicative practices (of which language is a part). Linguistic competence is outside the focus and scope of the model (Baker, 2011; 2015a); however, from the perspective of language learning and teaching this obviously needs addressing and cannot be ignored. Overall, ICA is commensurable to the previously discussed critical approaches to communicative and intercultural communicative competence. These view linguistic resources as adaptable and part of multilingual repertoires. Additionally, linguistic resources are intertwined with other modes, through multi- and transmodality, and communicative resources such as communicative and pragmatic strategies. EMF awareness is especially relevant with its characterisation of a conscious understanding of transcultural, transmodal and multilingual communication integrated into learners' actual communicative practices (Baker & Ishikawa, 2021; Ishikawa 2020; 2021). Similar notions have also previously been proposed in translanguaging theory and research (Canagarajah, 2013; Hawkins & Mori, 2018; Li, 2018). Of course, participants in intercultural and transcultural communication do not have complete freedom. ICA, EMF awareness and similar concepts also need to include an understanding of more normative linguistic and cultural notions, particularly around national cultures and standard language ideologies (Baker & Ishikawa, 2021). To paraphrase the quotation from Baker and Sangiamchit (2019: 471) in Section 3, L2 learners and users need to simultaneously acknowledge the power of names and labels while attempting to critically explore the power structures this naming creates.

Finally, a number of empirical studies have explored the relevance of ICA to language education and intercultural development. These include Baker (2012; 2015a) in Thailand, Yu and Van Maele (2018) in China, Kusumaningputri and Widodo (2018) in Indonesia, Abdzadeh and Baker

(2020) in Iran, and Humphreys and Baker (2021) in Japan. In each of the studies, the relevance of ICA in understanding and documenting students' knowledge, skills and attitudes to intercultural communication was demonstrated. Moreover, development of ICA either through teaching interventions or experience of intercultural interactions (e.g. study abroad) was also shown. However, this development was typically from basic cultural awareness (level 1) to advanced cultural awareness (level 2). There was much less evidence of learners developing intercultural or transcultural awareness (level 3) through formal language education. With the exception of Kusumaningputri and Widodo (2018), advanced intercultural awareness seemed to have been developed by L2 language users outside the classroom (e.g. Baker, 2012; 2015a; Humphreys & Baker, 2021). These studies will be outlined in more detail in Section 5 when exploring the pedagogic implications of ICA.

4.6 Conclusion

In this section we have explored a fundamental concept in applied linguistics and language teaching – communicative competence. If the aim of teaching and learning an L2 is to engage in communication through that L2, then this is clearly an appropriate goal. However, as argued throughout this Element, most communication through an L2 is intercultural and transcultural communication and communicative competence, as conceived in applied linguistics, is not sufficient for this. The focus on monolingual native speaker L1 language norms and communities is neither relevant nor appropriate for L2 users of a language. A wider range of competencies is needed which fully incorporates the knowledge, skills and attitudes needed for successful intercultural and transcultural communication. In terms of language, this means making multilingualism core and preparing users for translanguaging processes. Equally important to these processes are other communicative modes that accompany linguistic resources through multimodality and transmodal practices. Alongside linguistic and multimodal resources are a range of communicative and pragmatic strategies that are also crucial for successful interactions. Furthermore, these resources and strategies need to be embedded in a wider set of competencies and awareness related to processes of intercultural and transcultural communication and engagement with diverse communities. This may include the knowledge, skills and attitudes associated with the *savoirs* (Byram, 1997; 2021) such as skills of discovery, interpretation, relation, interaction and critical cultural awareness. However, it is important that these are related to interaction across multiple cultural groupings from the local, to the national, and the global, with national cultures viewed as one scale among many. There also needs to be an awareness of the processes of intercultural and transcultural communication whereby borders between cultures, languages and modes can be transgressed and transcended and emergent communicative and other cultural practices created in situ. What this might entail has been outlined through notions such as ICA (Baker, 2015a) and EMF awareness (Baker & Ishikawa, 2021; Ishikawa, 2020) which, while developed in relation to ELF, are likely to be relevant to any languages used in multilingual and multicultural settings. Moreover, all of this knowledge and these skills need to be employed flexibly in a manner relevant to each interaction; there will be no one set of strategies or skills that are appropriate to all communicative settings. Finally, ideologies and power relationships are relevant to all communication, including intercultural and transcultural, and there needs to be an awareness of the role of standard language and national culture ideologies, as well as alternatives that challenge them. Evidently, this is a wider range of knowledge, skills and attitudes than that typically addressed in language teaching. How this might be incorporated into pedagogy will be the subject of the next section.

5 Intercultural and Transcultural Language Education

5.1 Introduction

Throughout this Element we have explored the interlinked nature of language and culture with language use viewed as a cultural practice. Yet, at the same time, the variability of the connections between particular linguistic resources and cultural practices and references has been underscored. This means that the relationship between language and culture is more complex and diverse than the essentialist national language and culture correlation typical in language teaching. Furthermore, learning and use of an L2 has been approached as an intercultural process involving engagement with diverse communities and cultural practices. Transcultural communication was also proposed as an addition to intercultural communication to account for the manner in which languages are used in fluid ways to create and reference cultural practices that may not be easily assigned to any one cultural group. Thus, learning and using an L2 is seen as a process involving multilingual, multimodal and multicultural resources in translingual, transmodal and transcultural processes. Such a holistic view of communication entails a range of competencies much wider than those traditionally conceived of in language teaching under communicative competence. As outlined in Section 4, knowledge, skills and attitudes related to the processes of intercultural and transcultural communication are fundamental to successful communication through an L2. In this section, we consider the implications of this for language teaching and learning.

The section begins with a brief overview of traditional approaches to teaching language and culture in 'foreign' language teaching. It is recognised that culture has long been part of language teaching, but it has typically been treated in an uncritical essentialist manner that does not match the intercultural and transcultural reality of much L2 use. Additionally, the gap between research, policy and practice as regards teaching culture and intercultural communication is noted. Next, a number of contemporary approaches which highlight key themes in intercultural language education are discussed such as critical perspectives, process orientations, expansions of communicative competence and de-centring the native speaker. This leads into a more focussed discussion of intercultural awareness (ICA) and intercultural citizenship education as approaches well-suited to the needs of intercultural and transcultural communication. Throughout this section, the term intercultural language education will be frequently used as intercultural is a more commonly understood term in the field. Nonetheless, the final section will draw together the themes discussed throughout this Element in proposing a transcultural language education approach. As with other sections of this Element, many of the examples will be taken from research on English language use, particularly ELF and ELT, due to the large number of English users and learners and the correspondingly extensive research. However, this is not to suggest that there is anything exclusive about English or that the proposals would not be equally relevant to other languages used and learnt for intercultural and transcultural communication.

5.2 Traditional Approaches to Teaching Culture and Language

As previously noted, culture has in one way or another always been an element of language teaching. In the 'foreign' language tradition, the language was learnt to communicate with and learn the culture of the 'other'. In particular, the literature of other cultures has been a central part of foreign language education for centuries as a means to learn both the foreign language and culture (Risager, 2007). However, since the 1990s the intercultural dimensions have come to the fore with a growing number of publications and research projects focussed on intercultural language education (Risager, 2007). The increased interest in the links between culture and language teaching are perhaps most apparent in language education policies which frequently contain references to culture and the intercultural. The original formulation of the highly influential Common European Framework of Reference for Languages (CEFR), whose reach extends far beyond Europe, drew specifically on Byram's (1997) ICC model (Council of Europe, 2001). This has been further extended in the updated 2018 version which now adds 'pluricultural competence' and seeks to 'promote plurilingual and intercultural education' www.coe.int/en/web/common-european-framework-reference-languages/home. In relation to national policies, the Modern Languages Association of America (MLA) makes multiple references to culture, the connections between culture, language and community, and intercultural communication (Glisan, 2012). Similar policies are found in other Anglophone settings such as Australia (Scarino & Liddicoat, 2009) and New Zealand (Newton et al., 2009). Taking two examples from Asia, in China the Chinese National English Curriculum contains a section on cultural awareness (Ministry of Education, 2011) and in Thailand 'language and culture' is one of the four basic strands of the Basic Education Core Curriculum B.E. 2551 (OBEC, 2008). However, in many of these policies there is still a focus on the national scale above the intercultural and transcultural. For instance, while the MLA guidelines refer to transcultural communication, they also contain multiple references to 'target' cultures and languages (Mori & Sanuth, 2018). Likewise, tensions between intercultural and national 'native speaker' perspectives and wording in policies have been noted in relation to China (Liu, 2016) and Thailand (Ra & Baker, 2021). This focus on the national scale is perhaps to be expected in government policies which are always likely to promote the primacy of the national scale, but it is more concerning when it appears in policies from language associations such as the MLA.

In addition to tensions between the national and intercultural paradigms in language education policies, there are also questions about the extent to which these policies are translated into classroom teaching, especially given the well-known gap between policy and practice. Studies have repeatedly shown teachers failing to incorporate cultural and intercultural elements into classroom teaching or approaching it in an ad hoc, inconsistent and/or superficial manner (e.g. Brunsmeier, 2017; Driscoll et al., 2013; Luk, 2012; Sercu et al., 2005; Snodin, 2016; Young & Sachdev, 2011). This is unsurprising given the lack of clear and consistent guidance in language education policies. Furthermore, intercultural communication is not usually a core part of teacher education, especially compared to aspects such as grammar and pronunciation (Kelly, 2012). Although, it should also be noted that intercultural communication is often a feature of postgraduate level programmes in applied linguistics and language teaching which may eventually have a 'trickle down' influence on wider teaching practices. Moreover, while there are now many proposals for intercultural education approaches, there is much less research on 'uptake and perceived applicability of this [intercultural] approach' (Young & Sachdev, 2011: 83). Language teachers are also frequently under pressure to deliver more than can realistically be fitted into class time. Without clear guidance and support, even if teachers are interested in intercultural education, they are unlikely to be able to incorporate it systematically and in-depth into their classroom (Liu, 2016). This is further exacerbated by the pressure to teach to exams which rarely, if ever, include intercultural communication in assessment. All of these factors result in the frequent marginalisation of intercultural communication within the language classroom where it becomes the 'fifth skill' (Kramsch, 1993) to be addressed as an optional 'extra' after the other four skills of speaking, listening, writing and reading. Yet by marginalising intercultural education in this way, teachers are often unwittingly ignoring the most important aspects of the learners' needs and motivations, which are to engage in intercultural communication.

Alongside the lack of uptake of intercultural teaching in classroom practices is the issue that, when culture and the intercultural is dealt with in the classroom, it is often in a stereotyped and essentialist manner. By far the most common approach is cross-cultural style comparisons between national cultures focussing on festivals, food and touristic images (Baker, 2015b). This essentialist approach is exemplified through the textbooks that form a core part of language teaching and typically approach culture in a superficial and stereotyped way (see Canale, 2021). For instance, Gray's (2010) in-depth analysis of the cultural content of ELT course books over forty years illustrated a limited range of cultural representations, a 'native-speaker' focus and an absence of locally relevant issues. Similarly, four studies of the cultural content of leading ELT course books come to similar conclusions despite being separated by twenty years. Jin and Cortazzi (1998), Vettorel (2010; 2018) and Rose and Galloway (2019) all report that culture was integrated into texts in a superficial and stereotyped manner, focussing on national scales, native speakers and simplistic target language–culture correlations. Furthermore, this national scale cultural content is often based on the intuition of material writers, rather than any systematic approach to intercultural language education. In the case of ELT materials, this typically results in a restricted white, middle-class, male and monolingual image of 'other' cultures (Baker, 2015a; Hall, 2013; Leung, 2005). Some recent textbooks have attempted to adopt a more international perspective (e.g. Clanfield, 2019) through, for example, the inclusion of 'authentic' interactions with 'non-native' speakers of English. Yet, closer examination reveals a continued bias towards 'native' English norms and Anglophone cultures with intercultural communication and diverse uses of English given much less space (Baker, 2015a; Dewey, 2015; Galloway, 2018; Rose & Galloway, 2019). In sum, while culture has long been a part of language teaching, it has typically been a marginal aspect and treated in an essentialist and superficial manner with little in-depth intercultural or transcultural engagement.

5.3 Contemporary Approaches to Intercultural Language Education

As a response to the limitations of traditional methods to intercultural education in language classrooms, there are a range of current approaches that attempt to integrate the intercultural dimension into language teaching in a systematic and non-essentialist manner. In this section the fundamental features of these will be outlined and evaluated; however, it is important to note that there is no suggestion that there is a single methodology or approach that would be appropriate in all settings. Indeed, as with language education in general, there has been a consensus that we need to adopt a post-methods perspective (Kumaravadivelu, 2012) where local contexts and stakeholders are given primacy over teaching methodologies. This is equally applicable to the selection of cultural content and the teaching of intercultural communication processes which need to be approached flexibly and in a way that is relevant to the needs and interests of teachers and students (Kirkpatrick, 2011; Kumaravadivelu, 2008). Following a post-methods perspective also entails a shift in teaching from a focus on *products* (e.g. knowledge of particular linguistic forms and cultural practices) to a focus on the *processes* of communication. Learners can never be prepared with knowledge of all the diverse linguacultural backgrounds of their potential interlocutors and the correspondingly variable linguistic and cultural practices they will encounter in intercultural and transcultural communication. Therefore, learners need to be made aware of the processes of intercultural and transcultural communication so that they can successfully adapt their linguistic and other communicative resources to each instance of communication. This does not entail a rejection of teaching linguistic and cultural products such as knowledge of grammar, vocabulary and pronunciation as well as information about other cultures. However, following what Dewey (2012) terms a 'post-normative' perspective, these should be presented in classrooms as examples of communicative resources that need adaptation to particular situations with no one set of communicative resources viewed as 'correct' or 'best'. Thus, all knowledge becomes provisional and open to further exploration and revision. As Canagarajah states in relation to performative competence (Section 4.4), 'competence isn't constituted of the *what*, but of the *how* of communication' (2013: 174).

Underpinning many attempts to develop non-essentialist approaches to intercultural language education have been critical perspectives on language, culture and identity which aim to challenge dominant discourses (e.g. Holliday, 2011; Kramsch, 2009; 2021; Piller, 2017; Zhu, 2019). Phipps and Guilherme describe such a critical pedagogy as 'a critical use of language(s), a critical approach to one's own and other cultural backgrounds and a critical view of intercultural interaction' (2004: 3). Piller (2017) suggests that teachers and learners should allow time to explore and challenge prevailing, hegemonic discourses of culture, especially at the national scale. Similarly, Kramsch argues for a post-structuralist and post-modernist language education that 'will require developing learners' interpretative abilities, sensitivity to context and appreciation of symbolic complexity' (2021: 203). To achieve this Kramsch proposes space and time to share thoughts and experience beyond the traditional structuralist syllabi (Kramsch, 2021: 236). Guilherme (2012; 2020) also emphasises the importance of space for teachers and students to reflect on their own experiences of intercultural communication and the complexity and diversity of those experiences. Another key theme in critical approaches is action and change with learners expected to actively engage in intercultural communication that results in change in themselves. As Liddicoat and Scarino write, '[a]n intercultural perspective implies the transformational engagement of the learner in the act of learning. The goal of learning is to decenter learners from their preexisting assumptions and practices and to develop an intercultural identity through engagement with an additional culture' (2013: 28–9). The role of intercultural language education in action and change for both individuals and communities has been crucial in recent thinking and is returned to when discussing intercultural citizenship education (Section 5.3.2).

A core feature of attempts to rethink intercultural language education has been an expansion of traditional notions of communicative competence in language teaching. As discussed in Section 4, in addition to linguistic competence, knowledge, skills and attitudes needed for intercultural communication are also included. Byram's (1997; 2021) intercultural communicative competence (ICC) is probably the most influential model. For Byram, intercultural competence is added to linguistic, sociolinguistic and discourse competence to fully account for the intercultural nature of L2 use. This intercultural competence consists of the five *savoirs*: attitudes (*savoir être*); knowledge (*savoirs*); skills of interpreting and relating (*savoir comprendre*); skills of discovery and interaction (*savoir apprendre/faire*); and critical cultural awareness/political education (*savoir s'engager*). As previously noted, ICC is a pedagogic model and the *savoirs* are presented as competences to be integrated into classroom practices, curriculum and assessment. This enables learners to advance their understanding of intercultural communication and the relationships between cultures and languages as they develop their L2. The relevance of ICC to pedagogy has been extensively investigated at multiple levels from primary to higher education and in diverse settings across the globe, often with positive outcomes (e.g. Byram & Fleming, 1998; Byram et al., 2001; Feng et al., 2009). However, the relevance of ICC for preparing learners for the complexity and diversity of transcultural communication has been questioned (Baker, 2015a). While current conceptions have made clear that ICC's focus is not only national scale culture and language correlations (Byram, 2021), the 'intercultural line' (Holliday, 2011) between 'our' culture and a 'foreign' culture is still maintained. In transcultural communication, linguistic and cultural resources may not be easily associated with any particular group, national or otherwise, and boundaries such as 'ours' or 'foreign' become blurred. Other more critical approaches to competence such as symbolic competence (Kramsch, 2009; 2011), performative competence (Canagarajah, 2013) and intercultural awareness (ICA) (Baker, 2011; 2015a) may be more appropriate (see Section 4). As yet, though, these approaches have not been investigated in classroom practices to the same extent as ICC. Nonetheless, classroom research on ICA is beginning to emerge and will be evaluated in the following section.

Closely linked to the expansion of communicative competence has been the replacement of the inappropriate native speaker model in language teaching with a model that incorporates the competencies and awareness needed for intercultural and transcultural communication. The competencies of an idealised monolingual and monocultural native speaker (as in communicative competence) are of questionable relevance to the multilingual and multicultural nature of intercultural and transcultural communication. Thus, the intercultural speaker who possesses the competences outlined in ICC is central to the model (Byram, 2008; 2021). The intercultural speaker also involves an attitudinal and motivational dimension including positive attitudes to difference, motivation to engage with 'others' and the ability to 'de-centre' and relativise one's own beliefs and practices. This, Byram argues, is the model that learning and teaching should orientate towards. Similar ideas are also proposed in critical intercultural education approaches. For example, Canagarajah (2013), when discussing performative competence, uses the term translinguals to refer to communicators who are able to flexibly employ their multilingual repertoires, negotiate form and meaning, and approach communication as a process. However, the replacement of the native speaker with an intercultural speaker (or similar notion) does not necessarily entail a radical shift in pedagogy. Many teachers are already multilingual and they can therefore better draw on their own experiences and competences in teaching rather than deferring to idealised native speakers of the 'target' language and culture. Moreover, the intercultural speaker provides an attainable model for learners which they can see both in their teachers but also outside the classroom where there are likely to be many examples of successful multilingual users of the language they are learning, especially for global languages such as English.

Many of the features of non-essentialist approaches to intercultural language education (a focus on process, criticality, expanded views of intercultural/communicative competence and the replacement of the native speaker model) have been incorporated into current thinking and research on teaching English as a global lingua franca. While there is not necessarily anything unique about English and ELT, the huge scale on which it is taught and used around the world has resulted in a correspondingly large amount of research exploring pedagogic changes. From the beginning of ELF research, there has been a critical approach to the dominant discourses of language teaching around native speakerism and 'target' language and culture correlations. Scholars argued for a recognition of the inherent variability of L2 use and multilingual intercultural communicators as the goal in teaching (e.g. Jenkins, 2000; 2007; Seidlhofer, 2001). Furthermore, there are a growing number of studies from an ELF and Global Englishes perspective that have explored teaching approaches which replace the traditional focus on Anglophone cultures with more locally relevant cultural references, as well as recognising the fluid links between languages and cultures (e.g. Crowther & De Costa, 2017; Galloway & Rose, 2018; Hino & Oda, 2015; Kirkpatrick, 2011; Rose & Galloway, 2019; Snodin, 2016). Importantly, studies such as Galloway (2013) and Hino and Oda (2015) have reported positive reactions from both students and teachers to these alternative approaches to cultural and intercultural content and processes. In particular, EMF awareness (Baker & Ishikawa, 2021; Ishikawa, 2020; 2021) is an approach which combines critical awareness of language, culture and communication (see Section 4.4). In terms of pedagogy, it is designed with two core principles: '(1) providing students with experiences of EMF scenarios, and (2) encouraging their critical thinking about language and culture in reference to their experiences and in reference to published research' (Ishikawa, 2021). Findings from two studies of EMF awareness in EMI (English Medium Instruction) classes in Japan (one for English majors and another for international students) illustrated the students' positive evaluations of the courses and also a greater awareness of the processes of translanguaging, transmodality and transcultural communication (Ishikawa, 2021). In my own research, I have explored the links between intercultural language educations, Global Englishes and ELT through the notion of ICA (e.g. Baker, 2011; 2012; 2015a; 2015b). In the next section, we will consider ICA in detail as an example of how ELT (and language teaching in general) can be made relevant to language learners who will engage in intercultural and transcultural communication.

5.3.1 ICA and Intercultural Language Education

Section 4.5 expained ICA in detail so it will not be repeated here, but it should be reiterated that ICA was proposed as a model with two purposes: firstly, as a model of the knowledge, skills and attitudes used in successful intercultural and transcultural interactions; and secondly, as a potential pedagogic model in terms of structuring and documenting learners' development of intercultural and transcultural awareness. The twelve elements and three levels (basic cultural awareness, advanced cultural awareness and intercultural/transcultural awareness) serve as a useful heuristic in considering the types of activities and interactions that learners will need to engage in at different levels of development and the subsequent development of appropriate syllabi and pedagogic activities around these levels. Additionally, ICA can be used to understand development and progress through the levels by comparing learners' activities (e.g. intercultural interactions and class work) and responses to those activities (e.g. interviews and written responses) with the different elements at each level. A number of empirical studies have explored the pedagogic relevance of ICA in a variety of settings including Baker (2012b; 2015a) in Thailand, Yu and Van Maele (2018) in China, Kusumaningputri and Widodo (2018) in Indonesia, Abdzadeh and Baker (2020) in Iran, and Humphreys and Baker (2021) in Japan.

In my research, I have proposed a number of principles which can guide the development of ICA in the classroom (Baker, 2012a; 2012b; 2015a). These are organised around five strands (adapted from Baker, 2015a: 195–8).

1. **Exploring the complexity of local cultures**. Through exploring their own cultural backgrounds and communities, students can become more aware of the diversity of their own cultures which can then be applied to understanding the complexity of 'other' cultures. Even supposedly monolingual and monocultural classes typically contain a variety of heritage languages, religions, ethnicities and multicultural/multinational family backgrounds. Activities can include mini-ethnographic projects and class discussions describing local communities and cultural groups.

2. **Exploring cultural representations in language-learning materials**. Textbooks and other teaching materials offer a readily accessible source of cultural content. Although the presentation of culture and the intercultural in teaching materials is often essentialist, if explored critically, they can still be

useful. Students can consider what images of their own and other cultures are presented. They can reflect on how well this matches their own experiences and understandings, as well as what might be missing, thus, developing the ability to critically evaluate cultural representations and comparisons.

3. **Exploring cultural representations in the media and arts both in digital and 'traditional' mediums**. Language teaching has a long tradition of using literature to bring cultural content into the classroom, and this can include other media sources, such as movies, television, radio and music, as well as digital sources, such as news websites, social networking sites, blogs and podcasts. These mediums can be used to explore the complexity of 'target' cultures from a variety of perspectives. Furthermore, digital sources often provide examples of hybrid and fluid cultural forms and practices that are not connected to any specific national culture and so help develop higher levels of intercultural and transcultural awareness.

4. **Making use of cultural informants**. Local language teachers often have experiences of intercultural communication through the language being learnt, and they can share these with their students. 'Non-local' language teachers can share their understanding of their own 'foreign' cultural background and provide outsider perspectives on students' cultures. Such accounts will, of course, be highly subjective; but, provided this is acknowledged, they offer valuable personal accounts of intercultural and transcultural communication.

5. **Engaging in intercultural communication both face-to-face and digitally**. Experience of intercultural and transcultural communication is central to developing ICA and should, if possible, be integrated into teaching activities. Traditionally this has taken place through physical student exchanges and study abroad in the 'target culture'. However, for global languages used as a lingua franca, such as English, any setting where the language is used will be relevant. Indeed, it may be that international, multilingual and multicultural environments are most relevant in the development of ICA (see Humphreys & Baker, 2021). Moreover, in super-diverse urban centres with multilingual and multicultural populations or settings with large numbers of international tourists, there may be locally based opportunities to engage in intercultural and transcultural communication. Digital interactions provide an additional or alternative means of introducing intercultural and transcultural communication into a wider range of classrooms including those where physical interactions are not possible. This may be asynchronous email exchanges, blogs or text-based chat

rooms, but can also be synchronous chat, voice and video, or combinations of these in social networking sites such as Facebook. Equally important is space to reflect on experiences of intercultural and transcultural communication, giving learners the opportunity to explore and discuss what was more or less successful. Furthermore, even when intercultural interactions cannot be part of classroom teaching, it may still be possible to provide space for discussion of students' previous experiences outside the classroom.

These five strands offer examples and suggestions for how the intercultural dimensions can be incorporated into language classrooms in a non-essentialist manner, even when there are apparently limited opportunities. However, they are not presented as a teaching methodology or an exhaustive list that will be applicable in all contexts. Which strands to include and the details of how this will be done are best decided in local settings depending on relevance and needs.

A study at a Thai university used ICA and the five strands described above to develop an exploratory ten-week online course in intercultural awareness and Global Englishes for undergraduate English language majors (Baker, 2012; 2015a). Findings demonstrated that ICA can be used to structure a course and aid in the development of interculturally relevant materials. Feedback from students who took part in the course and teachers who helped in the delivery was largely very positive, especially in relation to the wider, non-Anglocentric content. However, there was still a preference for Anglophone cultural content among a minority of students and teachers. As regards development of ICA, most awareness appeared to be at levels 1 and 2, with students discussing and comparing their own and other cultures in both essentialist and non-essentialist ways. There appeared to be much less development of intercultural or transcultural awareness associated with fluid cultural and linguistic practices. However, due to the voluntary and short nature of the course (10–20 hours of study), it would be unrealistic to expect substantial development of ICA.

Building on the previous study (Baker, 2012; 2015a), Abdzadeh developed a ten-session course aimed at improving ICA in an Iranian ELT classroom (Abdzadeh, 2017; Abdzadeh & Baker, 2020). Due to the basic level of the students and their lack of intercultural experiences, it was decided to focus on the first two levels of ICA (basic and advanced cultural awareness) in development of the materials and activities. Similar to Baker's earlier study, the course received positive evaluation from the students. Moreover, findings documented improvements in students' levels of ICA moving from basic cultural awareness in the first half of the course to increased evidence of advanced cultural awareness in the second half, often in direct response to teaching activities. Unsurprisingly, given the focus on the first two levels of ICA, the shortness of the course and the basic level of the students, there was no evidence of inter-cultural or transcultural awareness. Nonetheless, like Baker (2012; 2015a), this study demonstrated the feasibility and value of ICA for intercultural language education.

Yu and Van Maele (2018) used ICA in the design of the teaching flow and for defining learning goals in order to integrate intercultural learning into an English reading course in a Chinese university. Similar to Abdzadeh and Baker (2020), the results indicated that the course had been successful in developing cultural awareness at levels 1 and 2 of ICA. However, Yu and Van Maele concluded that more time and further adjustments to the teaching activ-ities would be needed to reach more advanced levels. In Kusumaningputri and Widodo's (2018) study of an ELT class in an Indonesian university, they used digital photograph, mediated intercultural tasks as a way to develop ICA. In contrast to the previous studies, their findings illustrated more advanced devel-opment at level 3 of ICA where cultures and cultural identities were seen as fluid and adaptable (Kusumaningputri & Widodo, 2018: 59). Most recently, Humphreys and Baker (2021) used the three levels of ICA to document and understand the intercultural development of Japanese students taking part in short-term study abroad programmes. Although the findings predominantly illustrated students' development from level 1 to level 2 of ICA as the result of study abroad, there was some evidence of level 3 of ICA. However, in the few instances when this occurred, it was not clear if this was the result of students' previous experiences rather than study abroad, as no clear development between level 2 and 3 of ICA could be seen. Finally, while not an empirical study itself, Crowther and De Costa (2017) surveyed a number of empirical studies that incorporated the five strands of ICA in classroom pedagogy. They concluded that, together with the critical pedagogic insights from ELF research, ELT classrooms can successfully go beyond linguistic development and 'help foster the skills learners need to enter a globalized world with a goal of conviviality, in which they use their intercultural awareness to work in harmony with their fellow global citizens' (2017: 458).

In conclusion, current research investigating ICA in intercultural language education suggests it is relevant as both a means of developing intercultural syllabi, activities and materials, and as a way to document and measure inter-cultural development. However, the majority of studies to date have suggested that within language classrooms this development is typically confined to the lower levels of basic and advanced cultural awareness rather than intercultural and transcultural awareness. When evidence of intercultural and transcultural awareness has occurred, it is unclear if this is the result of formal education or students' experiences of intercultural interactions outside the classroom. Therefore, further studies with more advanced level students in a greater range of settings and over longer periods of time are needed.

5.3.2 Intercultural Citizenship and Intercultural Language Education

Another current approach to intercultural language education that combines many of the elements of critical pedagogy, intercultural competence and awareness is intercultural citizenship education. Intercultural citizenship is also sometimes referred to as global citizenship, and while global citizenship education has a longer history and a wider remit, intercultural citizenship is more common in relation to language education. Nonetheless, the two terms are frequently used synonymously and both will be used here. Intercultural and global citizenship is typically conceived as an expansion of citizenship beyond national borders that recognises the many ways we are now globally connected. Yet, how best to define the core features of intercultural citizenship is controversial and there are competing notions. In particular, neo-liberal conceptions are often related to networks which promote globally connected elites, focus on economic gains and further entrench a discourse of privilege for the centre and devalue the periphery (Aktas et al., 2017; De Costa 2016). Furthermore, intercultural citizenship is subject to various interpretations in different national education systems and by different stakeholders as illustrated by De Costa (2016) in Singapore, Han et al. (2017) in China and Sharkey (2018) in the US. However, within education theory, there is general agreement that the features of intercultural citizenship include a commitment to social justice through participation in and responsibility to communities at multiple scales from the local to the national and the global, as well as valuing and respecting diversity across these different communities (Byram et al., 2017; Gaudelli, 2016; Killick, 2013). As a result of the influence of globalisation on all aspects of education and the curriculum, and the wide scope of intercultural citizenship, it is argued that intercultural citizenship education should be incorporated into all subjects (Gaudelli 2016; Killick 2013). Yet, language education is an especially relevant medium in which to develop intercultural citizenship due to the focus on intercultural communication and 'other' cultures (Byram et al., 2017; Porto et al., 2018).

Within language education, Byram's (2008) definition of intercultural citizenship education has been extensively used and is particularly relevant to this discussion, since it draws directly on elements of ICC as well as relating to ICA. It is defined as:

1. Causing/ facilitating intercultural citizenship experience, and analysis and reflection on it and on the possibility of further social and/ or political activity – i.e. activity which involves working with others to achieve an agreed end.
2. Creating learning/ change in the individual: cognitive, attitudinal, behavioural change; change in self-perception; change in relationships with Others (i.e. people of a different social group); change that is based in the particular but is related to the universal.

(Byram, 2008: 187)

In intercultural citizenship education, 'activity', 'experience' and 'change' are central, giving it an action dimension which was missing from the model of ICC (Byram, 2021: 150) and less emphasised in ICA. It begins with the idea of engaging with intercultural citizenship experience and social/political (in the general sense of social issues) activity through 'working with others'. This, in turn, results in change in the learner which gives rise to subsequent changes in their relationships to 'others' and diverse social groups. Thus, intercultural citizenship education goes beyond the awareness raising of ICC and ICA and extends the practices dimensions through action and change.

Although intercultural citizenship is a new area of research in language education, empirical studies are beginning to emerge (e.g. Byram et al., 2017; Porto et al., 2018). There are a number of ways in which the intercultural communication experiences that form the foundation of intercultural citizenship education can be incorporated into classroom practices. Many of these were discussed in relation to ICA (Section 4.3.1), with online teletandem intercultural exchanges with language learners in other parts of the world a well-documented approach (e.g. Porto, 2014). Another approach is intercultural group work projects, such as mini-ethnographies investigating the linguistic and cultural complexity of specific communities both locally and in international settings. Byram et al. argue that such projects can 'create a sense of international identification with learners in the international project; challenge the "common sense" of each national group within the international project; develop a new "international" way of thinking *and acting* . . .; apply that new way to "know-ledge", to "self" and to "the world"' (2017: xxviii). Importantly, these approaches go beyond awareness raising and involve direct engagement and action with others and other communities.

Research, such as Fang and Baker (2018) and Baker and Fang (2021), has illustrated that, for many students, there is a strong link between language learning and developing an identity as an intercultural citizen. This is particularly relevant to English, given its role as a global lingua franca; for instance, a number of participants in Baker and Fang's (2021) study regarded the development of English proficiency and intercultural citizenship as going hand-in-hand. However, given that English is used as a lingua franca for intercultural communication, including in intercultural citizenship projects, it is crucial that critical approaches to language are adopted that recognise the multilingual settings in which English operates alongside other languages and where variability is the norm. Language teaching, thus, needs to prepare leaners for these multilingual and dynamic communicative scenarios. Approaches previously outlined from ELF and Global Englishes perspectives which are particularly relevant include exposing learners to different varieties and variable uses of English, discussions of English 'ownership' and what constitutes 'proficient' English use, as well as providing opportunities for learners to use English, and other linguistic resources, in variable and adaptable ways (e.g. Bayyurt & Akcan, 2015; Crowther & De Costa 2017; Fang & Ren, 2018; Rose & Galloway, 2019; Sifakis et al., 2018). Learners also need space to reflect on the links between language learning/use, intercultural communication and their identification with intercultural citizenship. Indeed, the intercultural citizen provides an empowering alternative identity and goal to the potentially disempowering and unattainable 'native speaker' model. Furthermore, this is equally relevant to language teachers who also need opportunities to reflect on their own use of English and the potential development of an intercultural citizen identity as a more relevant alternative to the much criticised model of the idealised native English speaker as teacher. This means that intercultural citizenship education and critical approaches to language should also be incorporated into teacher education (e.g. Palpacuer-Lee et al., 2018; Peck & Wagner, 2017; Sharkey, 2018). Currently though, as with intercultural education in general, studies such as Fang and Baker (2018) and Baker and Fang (2021) suggest that intercultural citizenship education is typically not part of students' language education experiences. Consequently, intercultural citizenship needs to be better integrated into pre-service and in-service teacher education, and more pedagogically focussed research is needed to explore relevant approaches and materials in a variety of classroom settings.

5.4 Conclusion: Transcultural Language Education

We are now in a position to draw together many of the different strands discussed in this section as regards language teaching and intercultural and transcultural communication. Firstly, it is worth repeating that learning and using an additional language is an intercultural process and needs to be recognised as such in pedagogy. However, it is important that we avoid essentialist perspectives that are based on idealised native speaker models of communication and simplistic national language and culture correlations. While the national scale has traditionally featured prominently in language teaching, and particularly ELT, it is more likely to hinder than help in intercultural and transcultural communication where the national scale is one of many and may not be of relevance at all. Instead, we need to acknowledge the multilingual, multimodal and multicultural resources and translanguaging, transmodal and transcultural processes that L2 use entails. Thus, more critical approaches should be adopted that recognise language learning as process rather than product orientated; expand communicative competence to incorporate the knowledge, skills and attitudes needed for intercultural and transcultural L2 communication; replace the native speaker model with the intercultural speaker and intercultural citizen; introduce perspectives that challenge dominant discourses of learners 'own' and 'other' cultures and languages; raise awareness of language, including standard language ideologies, multilingualism and translanguaging; and provide space for reflection and discussion of intercultural and transcultural experiences. This transcultural approach and how it contrasts with more traditional approaches to language teaching can be summarised in Table 1 below.

The overall aims of a transcultural pedagogy go beyond awareness raising (although this is still a crucial step) and include change in the learners that, in turn, results in action through learners' engagement with a diverse range of communities across cultural and linguistic boundaries. While a variety of suggested pedagogic approaches that may help to achieve these aims have been given in this section, especially in relation to ICA and intercultural citizenship education, there will be no single methodology that is relevant and appropriate in all settings. It must also be recognised that labels such as 'traditional' and 'transcultural' language teaching as presented in Table 1. are broad categorisations and simplifications of teaching approaches. In actual teaching practices, teachers are unlikely to neatly fall into one category or the other and may adopt different elements from both approaches depending on circumstances and preferences. Additionally, it is possible for teachers to make incremental changes towards a more transcultural approach without necessarily adopting all of the elements. Accordingly, although theory and research can help inform and inspire teachers, the details on how to incorporate aspects of a transcultural approach are best decided in local settings based on the needs and interests of teachers and students. Furthermore, just as transcultural research represented an addition to, rather than rejection of, intercultural communication research, so too does transcultural education, which builds on earlier intercultural language

Table 1 Transcultural language education

Traditional language teaching	Transcultural language teaching
National-scale standard language ideologies with national language varieties associated with national cultural characterisations	A critical approach to language, culture and identity that challenges dominant established discourses and recognises the global role of languages (e.g. English as a multilingua franca) for transcultural communication across and through borders
Communicative competence with a focus on linguistic and grammatical competence	Intercultural communicative competence (ICC) and awareness (ICA) including pragmatic competence and fostering positive attitudes to difference and 'others'
Native-speaker models	The intercultural speaker and intercultural citizen as models
Focus on linguistic products, such as grammar, vocabulary and pronunciation	Focus on processes of communication and adaptable use of communicative resources including awareness of multilingualism and translanguaging (e.g. English as a multilingua franca (EMF) awareness)
Endonormative, centre methodologies and approaches (often Anglocentric)	Teaching based on local contexts and cultures

(adapted from Baker & Ishikawa, 2021: 309)

education approaches. In particular, it draws together many of the features of critical perspectives but places greater emphasis on preparing learners for communication where linguistic and cultural boundaries are transcended and participants are not necessarily in between any specific cultural grouping.

Transcultural communication and transcultural language education are clearly new ideas and, to an extent, still 'works-in-progress'. Further empirical studies are needed to investigate both the relevance to communication and pedagogy. Nonetheless, in relation to teaching, many of the core features are already being investigated, as outlined previously, through notions such as ICA (e.g. Abzadeh & Baker, 2020; Baker, 2015a; Humphreys & Baker, 2021), EMF awareness (e.g. Ishikawa, 2020), intercultural citizenship education (e.g. Byram et al., 2017; Porto et al., 2018), and globally orientated ELT, such as

GELT approaches (e.g. Bayyurt & Akan, 2015; Fang & Ren, 2018; Galloway & Rose, 2018; Rose & Galloway, 2019). However, more empirical studies are needed at a wider range of levels, in more settings, for different languages, and especially in greater collaboration with teachers. It is hoped that transcultural language education will better prepare L2 users for the reality of communication in culturally and linguistically diverse settings and offer a more empowering pedagogy through placing L2 users and their experiences of intercultural and transcultural communication at the centre of teaching.

References

Abdzadeh, Y. (2017). Raising cultural awareness in Iranian English language classroom: can a tailored course make a difference? Unpublished PhD, University of Southampton.

Abdzadeh, Y., & Baker, W. (2020). Cultural awareness in an Iranian English language classroom: a teaching intervention in an interculturally 'conservative' setting. *Journal of English as a Lingua Franca, 9*(1), 57–80. doi:http://doi.org/10.1515/jelf-2020-2030

Aktas, F., Pitts, K., Richards, J. C., & Silova, I. (2016). Institutionalizing global citizenship: a critical analysis of higher education programs and curricula. *Journal of Studies in International Education, 21*(1), 65–80. doi:10.1177/1028315316669815

Appadurai, A. (1996). *Modernity at Large: Cultural Dimensions of Globalization.* Minneapolis; London: University of Minnesota Press.

Baker, W. (2009). The cultures of English as a lingua franca. *TESOL Quarterly, 43*(4), 567–92. doi:10.1002/j.1545-7249.2009.tb00187.x

Baker, W. (2011). Intercultural awareness: modelling an understanding of cultures in intercultural communication through English as a lingua franca. *Language and Intercultural Communication, 11*(3), 197–214. doi:10.1080/14708477.2011.577779

Baker, W. (2012). Using online learning objects to develop intercultural awareness in ELT: a critical examination in a Thai higher education setting. *British Council Teacher Development Research Papers.* Available at: www.teachingenglish.org.uk/publications (14 June 2020).

Baker, W. (2015a). *Culture and Identity through English as a Lingua Franca: Rethinking Concepts and Goals in Intercultural Communication.* Berlin: De Gruyter Mouton.

Baker, W. (2015b). Research into practice: cultural and intercultural awareness. *Language Teaching, 48*(1), 130–41.

Baker, W. (2018). English as a lingua franca and intercultural communication. In J. Jenkins, W. Baker, & M. Dewey (Eds.), *The Routledge Handbook of English as a Lingua Franca* (pp. 25–36). Abingdon, UK: Routledge.

Baker, W., & Fang, F. (2021). 'So maybe I'm a global citizen': developing intercultural citizenship in English medium education. *Language, Culture and Curriculum, 34*(1), 1–17. doi:10.1080/07908318.2020.1748045

Baker, W., & Ishikawa, T. (2021). *Transcultural Communication through Global Englishes.* Abingdon, UK: Routledge.

Baker, W., & Sangiamchit, C. (2019). Transcultural communication: language, communication and culture through English as a lingua franca in a social network community. *Language and Intercultural Communication, 19*(6), 471–87. doi:10.1080/14708477.2019.1606230

Bayyurt, Y., & Akcan, S. (Eds.). (2015). *Current Perspectives on Pedagogy for ELF*. Berlin: De Gruyter Mouton.

Billing, M. (1995). *Banal Nationalism*. London: Sage.

Blommaert, J. (2010). *The Sociolinguistics of Globalization*. Cambridge: Cambridge University Press.

Boas, F. (1911/1986). Language and thought. In J. M. Valdes (Ed.), *Culture Bound* (pp. 5–7). Cambridge: Cambridge University Press.

Brumfit, C. (2001). *Individual Freedom in Language Teaching: Helping Learners to Develop a Dialect of Their Own*. Oxford: Oxford University Press.

Brunsmeier, S. (2017). Primary teachers' knowledge when initiating intercultural communicative competence. *TESOL Quarterly, 51*(1), 143–55. https://doi.org/10.1002/tesq.327

Byram, M. (1997). *Teaching and Assessing Intercultural Communicative Competence*. Clevedon, UK: Multilingual Matters.

Byram, M. (2008). *From Foreign Language Education to Education for Intercultural Citizenship: Essays and Reflections*. Clevedon, UK: Multilingual Matters.

Byram, M. (2021). *Teaching and Assessing Intercultural Communicative Competence: Revisited*. Clevedon, UK: Multilingual Matters.

Byram, M., & Fleming, M. (Eds.). (1998). *Language Learning in Intercultural Perspective*. Cambridge: Cambridge University Press.

Byram, M., Golubeva, I., Han, H., & Wagner, M. (Eds.). (2017). *From Principles to Practice in Education for Intercultural Citizenship*. Bristol: Multilingual Matters.

Byram, M., Nichols, A., & Stevens, D. (Eds.). (2001). *Developing Intercultural Competence in Practice*. Clevedon, UK: Multilingual Matters.

Canagarajah, S. (2007). Lingua franca English, multilingual communities, and language acquisition. *The Modern Language Journal, 91*(5), 923–39.

Canagarajah, S. (2013). *Translingual Practice: Global Englishes and Cosmopolitan Relations*. London: Routledge.

Canale, G. (2021). The language textbook: representation, interaction & learning: conclusions. *Language, Culture and Curriculum, 34*(2), 199–206. doi:10.1080/07908318.2020.1797081

Canale, M. (1983). From communicative competence to communicative language pedagogy. In J. Richards & R. Schmidt (Eds.), *Language and Communication* (pp. 2–27). Harlow UK: Longman.

Canale, M., & Swain, M. (1980). Theoretical bases of communicative approaches to second language teaching and testing. *Applied Linguistics, 1*(1), 1–47.

Clifford, J. (1992). Travelling cultures. In L. Grossberg, C. Nelson, and L. Treichler. (Eds.), *Cultural Studies* (pp. 96–112). New York: Routledge.

Cogo, A. (2016). Conceptualizing ELF as a translanguaging phenomenon: covert and overt resources in a transnational workplace. *Waseda Working Papers in ELF, 5*, 1–17.

Cogo, A. (2018). ELF and multilingualism. In J. Jenkins, W. Baker, & M. Dewey (Eds.), *The Routledge Handbook of English as a Lingua Franca* (pp. 357–68). Abingdon, UK: Routledge.

Cook, V. (Ed.). (2002). *Portraits of the L2 User*. Clevedon, UK: Multilingual Matters.

Cook, V. (2008). Multi-competence: black hole or wormhole for second language acquisition research? In Z. H. Han (Ed.), *Understanding Second Language Process* (pp. 16–26). Clevedon, UK: Multilingual Matters.

Council of Europe. (2001). *Common European Framework of Reference for Languages: Learning, Teaching, Assessment*. Cambridge: Cambridge University Press.

Crowther, D., & De Costa, P. I. (2017). Developing mutual intelligibility and conviviality in the 21st century classroom: insights from English as a lingua franca and intercultural communication. *TESOL Quarterly, 51*(2), 450–60. doi:10.1002/tesq.341

De Costa, P. (2016). Constructing the global citizen: an ELF perspective. *Journal of Asian Pacific Communication, 26*(2), 238–59. doi:10.1075/japc.26.2.04dec

Deutscher, G. (2010). *Through the Language Glass: How Words Colour Your World*. London: William Heinemann.

Dewey, M. (2012). Towards a post-normative approach: learning the pedagogy of ELF. *Journal of English as a Lingua Franca, 1*(1), 141–70. doi:10.1515/jelf-2012-0007

Dewey, M. (2015). Time to wake up some dogs! Shifting the culture of language in ELT. In Y. Bayyurt & S. Akcan (Eds.), *Current Perspectives on Pedagogy for ELF* (pp. 121–34). Berlin: De Gruyter Mouton.

Dovchin, S., Sultana, S., & Pennycook, A. (2016). Unequal translingual Englishes in the Asian peripheries. *Asian Englishes, 18*(2), 92–108. doi:10.1080/13488678.2016.1171673

Driscoll, P., Earl, J., & Cable, C. (2013). The role and nature of the cultural dimension in primary modern languages. *Language, Culture and Curriculum, 26*(2), 146–60. doi:10.1080/07908318.2013.799675

Ehrenreich, S. (2009). English as a lingua franca in multinational corporations: exploring business communities of practice. In A. Mauranen & E. Ranta (Eds.), *English as a Lingua Franca: Studies and Findings* (pp. 126–51). Newcastle: Cambridge Scholars.

Ehrenreich, S. (2018). Communities of practice and English as a lingua franca. In J. Jenkins, W. Baker, & M. Dewey (Eds.), *The Routledge Handbook of English as a Lingua Franca*. Abingdon, UK: Routledge.

Everett, D. L. (2012). *Language: The Cultural Tool*. London: Profile.

Fang, F., & Baker, W. (2018). 'A more inclusive mind towards the world': English language teaching and study abroad in China from intercultural citizenship and English as a lingua franca perspectives. *Language Teaching Research*, *22*(5), 608–24. doi:10.1177/1362168817718574

Fang, F., & Ren, W. (2018). Developing students' awareness of global Englishes. *ELT Journal*, *72*(4), 384–94. doi:10.1093/elt/ccy012

Feng, A., Byram, M., & Fleming, M. (Eds.). (2009). *Becoming Interculturally Competent through Education and Training*. Bristol: Multilingual Matters.

Galloway, N. (2018). ELF and ELT teaching materials. In J. Jenkins, W. Baker, & M. Dewey (Eds.), *The Routledge Handbook of English as a Lingua Franca* (pp. 468–80). Abingdon, UK: Routledge.

Galloway, N., & Rose, H. (2018). Incorporating global Englishes into the ELT classroom. *ELT Journal*, *72*(1), 3–14. doi:10.1093/elt/ccx010

Garcia, O., & Kleyn, T. (Eds.). (2016). *Translanguaging with Multilingual Students*. Abingdon, UK: Routledge.

Gaudelli, W. (2016). *Global Citizenship Education: Everyday Transcendence*. Abingdon, UK: Routledge.

Gee, J. P. (2008). *Social Linguistics and Literacies: Ideology in Discourses*. Abingdon, UK: Routledge.

Geertz, C. (1973/2000). *The Interpretation of Cultures*. New York: Basic Books.

Gleick, J. (1998). *Chaos: Making a New Science*. London: Vintage.

Glisan, E. (2012). National Standards: research into practice. *Language Teaching*, *45*(4), 515–26.

Gray, J. (2010). *The Construction of English: Culture, Consumerism and Promotion in the ELT Global Coursebook*. Basingstoke, UK: Palgrave Macmillan.

Guilherme, M. (2012). Critical language and intercultural communication pedagogy. In J. Jackson (Ed.), *The Routledge Handbook of Language and Intercultural Communication* (pp. 357–71). Abingdon, UK: Routledge.

Guilherme, M. (2020). Intercultural responsibility: transnational research and glocal critical citizenship. In J. Jackson (Ed.), *The Routledge Handbook of*

Language and Intercultural Communication (2nd ed., pp. 343–60). Abingdon, UK: Routledge.

Guilherme, M., & Dietz, G. (2015). Difference in diversity: multiple perspectives on multicultural, intercultural, and transcultural conceptual complexities. *Journal of Multicultural Discourses*, *10*(1), 1–21. doi:10.1080/17447143.2015.1015539

Hall, C. (2013). Cognitive contributions to plurilithic views of English and other languages. *Applied Linguistics*, *34*(2), 211–31.

Hall, E. T. (1959). *The Silent Language*. New York: Doubleday Anchor.

Hall, E. T. (1966). *The Hidden Dimension*. New York: Doubleday Anchor.

Halliday, M. A. K. (1979). *Language as Social Semiotic*. Victoria: Edward Arnold.

Han, H., Li, S., Hongtao, J., & Yuqin, Z. (2017). Exploring perceptions of intercultural citizenship among English learners in Chinese universities. In M. Byram, I. Golubeva, H. Han, & M. Wagner (Eds.), *From Principles to Practice in Education for Intercultural Citizenship* (pp. 25–44). Bristol: Multilingual Matters.

Hannerz, U. (1996). *Transnational Connections: Culture, People, Places*. Abingdon, UK: Routledge.

Harris, R. (1998). Making sense of communicative competence. In R. Harris & G. Wolf (Eds.), *Integrational Linguistics* (pp. 27–45). Oxford: Elsevier.

Hawkins, M. R. (2018). Transmodalities and transnational encounters: fostering critical cosmopolitan relations. *Applied Linguistics*, *39*(1), 55–77. doi:10.1093/applin/amx048

Hawkins, M. R., & Mori, J. (2018). Considering 'trans-' perspectives in language theories and practices. *Applied Linguistics*, *39*(1), 1–8. doi:10.1093/applin/amx056

Hino, N., & Oda, S. (2015). Integrated practice in teaching English as an international language (IPTEIL): a classroom ELF pedagogy in Japan. In Y. Bayyurt & S. Akcan (Eds.), *Current Perspectives on Pedagogy for ELF* (pp. 35–50). Berlin: De Gruyter Mouton.

Hofstede, G. H. (1980). *Culture's Consequences: International Differences in Work-Related Values*. Beverly Hills: Sage.

Hofstede, G. H. (1991). *Cultures and Organizations: Software of the Mind*. London: McGraw Hill.

Holliday, A. (1999). Small cultures. *Applied Linguistics*, *20*(2), 237–64.

Holliday, A. (2011). *Intercultural Communication and Ideology*. London: Sage.

Holliday, A. (2013). *Understanding Intercultural Communication: Negotiating a Grammar of Culture*. Abingdon, UK: Routledge.

Humphreys, G., & Baker, W. (2021). Developing intercultural awareness from short-term study abroad: insights from an interview study of Japanese students. *Language and Intercultural Communication, 21*(2), 260-275. doi:10.1080/14708477.2020.1860997

Hymes, D. (1972). On communicative competence. In J. B. Pride & J. Holmes (Eds.), *Sociolinguistics* (pp. 269–93). Harmondsworth: Penguin.

Ishikawa, T. (2020). EMF awareness in the Japanese EFL/EMI context. *ELT Journal, 70*(4), 408–417. doi:10.1093/elt/ccaa037

Ishikawa, T. (2021). EMF and translanguaging in the Japanese EMI higher education context. In W. Tsou & W. Baker (Eds.), *English-Medium Instruction Translanguaging Practices in Asia: Theories, Frameworks and Implementation in Higher Education* (pp. 39–58). Cham: Springer.

Jenkins, J. (2000). *The Phonology of English as an International Language: New Models, New Norms, New Goals*. Oxford: Oxford University Press.

Jenkins, J. (2007). *English as a Lingua Franca: Attitude and Identity*. Oxford: Oxford University Press.

Jenkins, J. (2015). Repositioning English and multilingualism in English as a lingua franca. *Englishes in Practice, 2*(3), 49–85. doi:10.1515/eip-2015-0003

Jenkins, J. (2018). The future of English as a lingua franca? In J. Jenkins, W. Baker, & M. Dewey (Eds.), *The Routledge Handbook of English as a Lingua Franca* (pp. 594–605). Abingdon, UK: Routledge.

Jenkins, J., Baker, W., & Dewey, M. (Eds.). (2018). *The Routledge Handbook of English as a Lingua Franca*. Abingdon, UK: Routledge.

Jenkins, J., Cogo, A., & Dewey, M. (2011). Review of developments in research into English as a lingua franca. *Language Teaching, 44*(3), 281–315.

Jenks, C. J. (2018). Uncooperative lingua franca encounters. In J. Jenkins, W. Baker, & M. Dewey (Eds.), *The Routledge Handbook of English as a Lingua Franca* (pp. 279–292). Abingdon, UK: Routledge.

Jin, L., & Cortazzi, M. (1998). The culture the learner brings: a bridge or a barrier. In M. Byram & M. Fleming (Eds.), *Language Learning in Intercultural Perspective* (pp. 98–118). Cambridge: Cambridge University Press.

Kalocsai, K. (2014). *Communities of Practice and English as a Lingua Franca: A Study of Erasmus Students in a Central-European Context*. Berlin: DeGruyter Mouton.

Kelly, M. (2012). Second language teacher education. In J. Jackson (Ed.), *The Routledge Handbook of Language and Intercultural Communication* (pp. 409–421). London: Routledge.

Killick, D. (2013). Global citizenship, sojourning students and campus communities. *Teaching in Higher Education, 18*(7), 721–35. doi:10.1080/13562517.2013.836087

Kirkpatrick, A. (2010). *English as a Lingua Franca in ASEAN*. Hong Kong: Hong Kong University Press.

Kirkpatrick, A. (2011). English as an Asian lingua franca and the multilingual model of ELT. *Language Teaching, 44*(2), 212–224.

Kramsch, C. (1993). *Context and Culture in Language Teaching*. Oxford: Oxford University Press.

Kramsch, C. (1998). *Language and Culture*. Oxford: Oxford University Press.

Kramsch, C. (2009). *The Multilingual Subject*. Oxford: Oxford University Press.

Kramsch, C. (2011). The symbolic dimensions of the intercultural. *Language Teaching, 44*(3), 354–367.

Kramsch, C. (2021). *Language as Symbolic Power*. Cambridge: Cambridge University Press.

Kress, G. (2017). What is a mode?. In C. Jewitt (Ed.), *The Routledge Handbook of Multimodal Analysis* (Second ed., pp. 60–75). Abingdon, UK: Routledge.

Kress, G. R., & Van Leeuwen, T. (2001). *Multimodal Discourse: The Modes and Media of Contemporary Communication*. London: Arnold.

Kumaravadivelu, B. (2008). *Cultural Globalization and Language Education*. London: Yale University Press.

Kumaravadivelu, B. (2012). *Language Teacher Education for a Global Society: A Modular Model for Knowing, Analyzing, Recognizing, Doing, and Seeing*. Abingdon, Oxon, UK: Routledge.

Kusumaningputri, R., & Widodo, H. P. (2018). Promoting Indonesian university students' critical intercultural awareness in tertiary EAL classrooms: the use of digital photograph-mediated intercultural tasks. *System, 72*, 49–61. doi:https://doi.org/10.1016/j.system.2017.10.003

Larsen-Freeman, D. (2018). Complexity and ELF. In J. Jenkins, W. Baker, & M. Dewey (Eds.), *The Routledge Handbook of English as a Lingua Franca* (pp. 51–60). Abingdon, UK: Routledge.

Larsen-Freeman, D., & Cameron, L. (2008). *Complex Systems and Applied Linguistics*. Oxford: Oxford University Press.

Lave, J., & Wenger, E. (1991). *Situated Learning: Legitimate Peripheral Participation*. Cambridge: Cambridge University Press.

Leavitt, J. (2015). Linguistic relativity: precursors and transformations. In F. Sharifian (Ed.), *The Routledge Handbook of Language and Culture* (pp. 3–15). Abingdon, UK: Routledge.

Leung, C. (2005). Convivial communication: recontextualizing communicative competence. *International Journal of Applied Linguistics, 15*(2), 121–144.

Li, W. (2016). New Chinglish and the post-multilingualism challenge: translanguaging ELF in China. *Journal of English as a Lingua Franca*, *5*(1), 1–25.

Li, W. (2018). Translanguaging as a practical theory of language. *Applied Linguistics*, *39*(1), 9–30. doi: 10.1093/applin/amx039

Liddicoat, A., & Scarino, A. (2013). *Intercultural Language Teaching and Learning*. London: Wiley-Blackwell.

Liu, H. (2016). Language policy and practice in a Chinese junior high school from global Englishes perspective. Unpublished PhD thesis, University of Southampton.

Luk, J. (2012). Teachers' ambivalence in integrating culture with EFL teaching in Hong Kong. *Language Culture and Curriculum*, *25*(3), 249–264.

Mauranen, A. (2012). *Exploring ELF: Academic English Shaped by Non-Native Speakers*. Cambridge: Cambridge University Press.

Miller, J. H., & Page, S. E. (2007). *Complex Adaptive Systems: An Introduction to Computational Models of Social Life*. Princeton, N.J.; Oxford: Princeton University Press.

Ministry of Education (in the People's Republic of China). (2011). *English Curriculum Standards for Compulsory Education*. Beijing: People's Education Press.

Mori, J., & Sanuth, K. K. H. (2018). Navigating between a monolingual utopia and translingual realities: experiences of American learners of Yorùbá as an additional language. *Applied Linguistics*, *39*(1), 78–98. doi:10.1093/applin/amx042

Newfield, D. (2017). Transformation, transduction and the transmodal moment. In C. Jewitt (Ed.), *The Routledge Handbook of Multimodal Analysis* (Second ed., pp. 100–14). Abingdon, UK: Routledge.

Newton, J., Yates, E., Shearn, S., & Nowitzki, W. (2009). *Intercultural Communicative Language Teaching: Implications for Effective Teaching and Learning*. Wellington: Ministry of Education.

OBEC (Office of the Basic Education Commission). (2008). *Basic Education Core Curriculum: B.E. 2551*. Bangkok: Ministry of Education. Available at: www.ipst.ac.th/index.php (accessed 30 September 2020).

Palpacuer-Lee, C., Hutchison Curtis, J., & Curran, M. E. (2018). Stories of engagement: pre-service language teachers negotiate intercultural citizenship in a community-based English language program. *Language Teaching Research*, *22*(5), 590–607. doi:10.1177/1362168817718578

Peck, C., & Wagner, M. (2017). Understanding intercultural citizenship in Korea and the USA. In M. Byram, I. Golubeva, H. Han, & M. Wagner (Eds.), *From Principles to Practice in Education for Intercultural Citizenship* (pp. 159–180). Bristol: Multilingual Matters.

Pennycook, A. (2007). *Global Englishes and Transcultural Flows*. London: Routledge.

Phipps, A. M., & Guilherme, M. (2004). *Critical Pedagogy: Political Approaches to Language and Intercultural Communication*. Clevedon, UK: Multilingual Matters.

Piller, I. (2011). *Intercultural Communication: A Critical Introduction*. Edinburgh: Edinburgh University Press.

Piller, I. (2017). *Intercultural Communication: A Critical Introduction* (2nd ed.). Edinburgh: Edinburgh University Press.

Pitzl, M.-L. (2018a). *Creativity in English as a Lingua Franca: Idiom and Metaphor*. Berlin: DeGruyter Mouton.

Pitzl, M.-L. (2018b). Transient international groups (TIGs): exploring the group and development dimension of ELF. *Journal of English as a Lingua Franca*, 7(1), 25–58. doi: 10.1515/jelf-2018-0002

Porto, M. (2014). Intercultural citizenship education in an EFL online project in Argentina. *Language and Intercultural Communication*, 14(2), 245–261. doi:10.1080/14708477.2014.890625

Porto, M., Houghton, S. A., & Byram, M. (2018). Intercultural citizenship in the (foreign) language classroom. *Language Teaching Research*, 22(5), 484–498. doi:10.1177/1362168817718580

Pratt, M. L. (2008). *Imperial Eyes: Travel Writing and Transculturation* (2nd ed.). London: Routledge.

Ra, J. J., & Baker, W. (2021). Translanguaging and language policy in Thai higher education EMI programmes. In W. Tsou & W. Baker (Eds.), *English-Medium Instruction Translanguaging Practices in Asia: Theories, Frameworks and Implementation in Higher Education*. Cham, Switzerland: Springer.

Risager, K. (2006). *Language and Culture: Global Flows and Local Complexity*. Clevedon, UK: Multilingual Matters.

Risager, K. (2007). *Language and Culture Pedagogy*. Clevedon, UK: Multilingual Matters.

Risager, K. (2012). Linguaculture and transnationality: the cultural dimensions of language. In J. Jackson (Ed.), *The Routledge Handbook of Language and Intercultural Communication* (pp. 101–115). London: Routledge.

Rose, H. (2019). Dismantling the ivory tower in TESOL: a renewed call for teaching-informed research. *TESOL Quarterly*, 53(3), 895–905. doi:10.1002/tesq.517

Rose, H., & Galloway, N. (2019). *Global Englishes for Language Teaching*. Cambridge: Cambridge University Press.

Scarino, A., & Liddicoat, A. (2009). *Teaching and Learning Languages: A Guide*. Melbourne: Curriculum Corporation.

Scollon, R., Scollon, S. B. K., & Jones, R. H. (2012). *Intercultural Communication: A Discourse Approach* (3rd ed.). Chichester: Wiley-Blackwell.

Scollon, R., & Scollon, S. W. (2001). Discourse and intercultural communication. In D. Schiffrin, D. Tannen, & H. Hamilton (Eds.), *The Handbook of Discourse Analysis* (pp. 538–547). Oxford: Blackwell.

Seidlhofer, B. (2001). Closing a conceptual gap: the case for a description of English as a lingua franca. *International Journal of Applied Linguistics, 11* (2), 133–158.

Seidlhofer, B. (2011). *Understanding English as a Lingua Franca.* Oxford: Oxford University Press.

Seidlhofer, B. (2018). Standard English and the dynamics of ELF variation. In J. Jenkins, W. Baker, & M. Dewey (Eds.), *The Routledge Handbook of English as a Lingua Franca* (pp. 85–100). Abingdon, UK: Routledge.

Seidlhofer, B., & Widdowson, H. G. (2009). Accommodation and the idiom principle in English as a lingua franca. In K. Murata & J. Jenkins (Eds.), *Global Englishes in Asian Contexts: Current and Future Debates* (pp. 26–39). Basingstoke, UK: Palgrave Macmillan.

Sercu, L. et al. (2005). *Foreign Language Teachers and Intercultural Competence: An International Investigation.* Clevedon, UK; Buffalo, US: Multilingual Matters.

Sharkey, J. (2018). The promising potential role of intercultural citizenship in preparing mainstream teachers for im/migrant populations. *Language Teaching Research, 22*(5), 570–589. doi:10.1177/1362168817718577

Sifakis, N., Lopriore, L., Dewey, M., Bayyurt, Y., Vettorel, P., Cavalheiro, L., . . . Kordia, S. (2018). ELF-awareness in ELT: bringing together theory and practice. *Journal of English as a Lingua Franca, 7*(1), 155–209. doi:10.1515/jelf-2018-0008

Slobin, D. (1996). From 'thought and language' to 'thinking for speech'. In J. Gumperz & S. Levinson (Eds.), *Rethinking Linguistic relativity.* Cambridge: Cambridge University Press.

Snodin, N. S. (2016). Rethinking culture teaching in English language programmes in Thailand. *RELC Journal, 47*(3), 387–398. doi:10.1177/0033688215609231

Spitzberg, B. H., & Changnon, G. (2009). *Conceptualizing Intercultural Competence.* London: Sage.

Street, B. (1993). Culture is a verb. In D. Graddol, L. Thompson, & M. Byram (Eds.), *Culture and Language* (pp. 23–43). Clevedon, UK: Multilingual Matters / British Association of Applied Linguistics.

Sultana, S. (2016). Reconceptualisation of ELF (English as a lingua franca): virtual space in focus. *Journal of Asian Pacific Communication, 26*(2), 216–237. doi:10.1075/japc.26.2.03sul

Tomasello, M. (2008). *Origins of Human Communication*. Cambridge, Mass: Massachusetts Institute of Technology Press.

van Ek, J. A. (1986). *Objectives for Modern Language Learning*. Strasbourg: Council of Europe.

Vettorel, P. (2010). EIL/ELF and representation of culture in textbooks: only food, fairs, folklore and facts? In C. Gagliardi & A. Maley (Eds.), *EIL, ELF, Global English: Teaching and Learning Issues* (pp. 153–187). Bern: Peter Lang.

Vettorel, P. (2014). *ELF in Wider Networking: Blogging Practices*. Berlin: De Gruyter Mouton.

Vettorel, P. (2018). ELF and communication strategies: are they taken into account in ELT materials? *RELC Journal, 49*(1), 58–73. doi:10.1177/0033688217746204

Welsch, W. (1999). Transculturality: the puzzling form of cultures today. In M. Featherstone & S. Lash (Eds.), *Spaces of Culture: City, Nation, World* (pp. 194–213). London: Sage.

Wenger, E. (1998). *Communities of Practice: Learning, Meaning, and Identity*. Cambridge: Cambridge University Press.

Whorf, B. (1939/1956). The relation of habitual thought and behavior to language. In J. Carroll (Ed.), *Language, Thought and Reality – Selected Writings of Benjamin Lee Whorf*. Cambridge, Mass: Massachusetts Institute of Technology Press.

Widdowson, H. G. (2012). ELF and the inconvenience of established concepts. *Journal of English as a Lingua Franca, 1*(1), 5–26.

Wierzbicka, A. (1997). *Understanding Cultures through Their Key Words: English, Russian, Polish, German, and Japanese*. Oxford: Oxford University Press.

Wierzbicka, A. (2006). *English: Meaning and Culture*. Oxford: Oxford University Press.

Williams, R. (2014). *Keywords: A Vocabulary of Culture and Society*. London: Fourth Estate.

Young, T. J., & Sachdev, I. (2011). Intercultural communicative competence: exploring English language teachers' beliefs and practices. *Language Awareness, 20*(2), 81–98.

Young, T. J., & Sercombe, P. (2010). Communication, discourses and interculturality. *Language and Intercultural Communication, 10*(3), 181–8.

Yu, Q., & van Maele, J. (2018). Fostering intercultural awareness in a Chinese English reading class. *Chinese Journal of Applied Linguistics, 41*(3), 357–375.

Zhu, H. (2019). *Exploring Intercultural Communication: Language in Action* (2nd ed.). Abingdon, UK: Routledge.

Zhu, H., & Li, W. (2016). 'Where are you really from?': nationality and ethnicity talk (NET) in everyday interactions. *Applied Linguistics Review, 7* (4), 449–470. doi: 10.1515/applirev-2016-0020

Cambridge Elements ≡

Language Teaching

Heath Rose

Linacre College, University of Oxford

Heath Rose is an Associate Professor of Applied Linguistics at the University of Oxford. At Oxford, he is course director of the MSc in Applied Linguistics for Language Teaching. Before moving into academia, Heath worked as a language teacher in Australia and Japan in both school and university contexts. He is author of numerous books, such as Introducing Global Englishes, The Japanese Writing System, Data Collection Research Methods in Applied Linguistics, and Global Englishes for Language Teaching. Heath's research interests are firmly situated within the field of second language teaching, and include work on Global Englishes, teaching English as an international language, and English Medium Instruction.

Jim McKinley

University College London

Jim McKinley is an Associate Professor of Applied Linguistics and TESOL at UCL, Institute of Education, where he serves as Academic Head of Learning and Teaching. His major research areas are second language writing in global contexts, the internationalisation of higher education, and the relationship between teaching and research. Jim has edited or authored numerous books including the Routledge Handbook of Research Methods in Applied Linguistics, Data Collection Research Methods in Applied Linguistics, and Doing Research in Applied Linguistics. He is also an editor of the journal, System. Before moving into academia, Jim taught in a range of diverse contexts including the US, Australia, Japan and Uganda.

About the Series

This Elements series aims to close the gap between researchers and practitioners by allying research with language teaching practices, in its exploration of research-informed teaching, and teaching-informed research. The series builds upon a rich history of pedagogical research in its exploration of new insights within the field of language teaching.

Cambridge Elements ≡

Language Teaching

Printed in the United States
by Baker & Taylor Publisher Services